WHY I AM
A
SPIRITUALIST

by

ADA A. McKAY

CON-PSY PUBLICATIONS

First Edition

© Ada A.McKay
2007

Published by

CON-PSY PUBLICATIONS

P.O. BOX 14,
GREENFORD,
MIDDLESEX, UB6 0UF.

ISBN 978 1 898680 44 4

TABLE OF CONTENTS.

ACKNOWLEDGEMENTS.

I would like to thank my friend Joyce Marchant who was the first person to read the finished manuscript and who pointed out some grammatical errors as well as helping to identify some of the quotations. During my researches for the book I made great use of the Postal Lending Library (for Spiritualists) which is run by Mary Malcolmson and I would like to thank her for supplying me with books and other materials. My neighbour and friend George Forsyth took the photo of me which has been used on the front cover and I am grateful for his photographic skills. Finally, I would like to thank Mr Ray Taylor of Con-Psy Publications for his help and encouragement in guiding a very inexperienced author through the process of getting her book published.

To

my mother and father

who, from the Next World,
continue to give me their love,
help and encouragement.

CHAPTER 1
WHAT IS SPIRITUALISM?

Spiritualism is three things. It is a RELIGION, (because Spiritualists believe in God.) It is a SCIENCE, (because we can prove the reality of the next world) and it is a CODE Of CONDUCT, (about how to live your life according to the Laws of God.)

First and foremost it is a RELIGION — yes it is, and I have encountered some pretty weird ideas about it! Some people even think that we worship the Devil! They are afraid to attend a Spiritualist meeting because they think that the tables will tilt and ghostly apparitions will appear. Now I would consider myself to be someone of a nervous disposition so if anything "spooky" happened at spiritualist meetings I would be the very last person to go to one. Here is what a typical Sunday morning service in a Spiritualist Church is like.

At my church we start off by reading out a list of names of all those we know who are sick and we have a minute's silence when we send out healing thoughts for these people and we never forget the Animal Kingdom. We sing a hymn, the visiting medium will give a prayer, a short reading is given by the presiding officer on the platform. Such a reading will be taken from a book on Spiritualism or perhaps it will be a poem by someone like Helen Steiner Rice. Another hymn during which the collection is taken. The visiting medium will then give a short talk about Spiritualism and very often he or she will mention current world events that we are all concerned about. The next part of the service is then concerned with communication between the two worlds and to "welcome" our loved ones from the next world we "raise the vibrations" by singing a rousing hymn. The visiting medium will now start her demonstration of clairvoyance. Anything up to 8 messages will be relayed from loved ones in the next world. There is then a closing hymn and prayer and the usual church announcements about future events such as healing sessions, classes for those who want to learn more about the movement, social events such as a coffee morning or names needed for an annual Christmas meal etc. There is no drawing of curtains and sitting in a darkened room and in fact the only time the curtains are ever drawn is to screen out the over bright sunshine which is dazzling our eyes. We do not consider any one day as

HOLY and services can be held on any day of the week but a Sunday service (morning and evening) is usual as this is when most people are able to attend.

Spiritualism is a religion which believes in God but unlike orthodox religions there is no Spiritualist Creed or Bible. Spiritualism does not have articles of faith which it insists upon its followers believing and accepting. However it does have its own philosophy of belief and this is summed up in what is known as the "Seven Principles of Spiritualism." These principles were given to the pioneering Victorian medium Emma Hardinge Britten in 1871 by Robert Owen, the great social reformer after he had passed to the next world. The principles are as follows:-

1. The Fatherhood of God.
2. The Brotherhood of Man.
3. Communion of Spirits and the Ministry of Angels.
4. The Continuous Existence of the Human Soul.
5. Personal Responsibility.
6. Compensation and Retribution hereafter for all the good and evil deeds done on earth.
7. Eternal progress open to every human soul.

Knowledge of these principles rapidly spread throughout the movement and when the Spiritualist National Union (SNU) was founded in 1902 the principles formed an important part of its Memorandum of Association although we do allow for freedom of interpretation. One of our most respected guides and teachers from the next world is called Silver Birch. He says that you must not accept any teaching without first considering it, pondering on it and reflecting. Never do anything which your reason rejects or which is foreign to your commonsense. Many who criticize Spiritualism have never read a book on the subject or attended a Spiritualist meeting. Spiritualism is not a religion which forces itself upon you and which tells you that you cannot do this and you cannot do that or, unless you do this and do that you cannot survive. Unlike other religions Spiritualism does not ask for a blind acceptance of faith in its teachings. We do not have rituals, we don't use prayers which are recited by memory without any thought being given to the actual meaning and Spiritualists do not accept one creed to the exclusion of others. In every religion there is truth.

As well as being a religion Spiritualism is also a SCIENCE. All religions believe in eternal life following death but Spiritualism is the only religion that can prove the existence of the next world and offer evidence of life after death. We are the only church to make contact with those in the next world. This proof and evidence is given to us through mediums. A medium is someone able to see and hear the so-called "dead." Many people think that it is not right to "Disturb the Dead." No medium can call up the dead. Mediums can only communicate with those who choose to come. Those who make contact do so because they want to. They want to assure those they love that they are still there. There have always been mediums going right back to Abraham who was chosen to work for God. He heard voices and saw angels. All the great prophets recorded in the Bible were mediums. The Bible is full of stories about how they passed on information from the Spirit realms to those on earth. (eg Elisha's prophecy in the Book of Kings about the price of food. 2nd Kings 7:1) The old religions are full of spiritualist experiences but when the churches came to power they persecuted the mediums because they wanted to suppress the truth. Mediums have been murdered over the centuries. Joan of Arc was a medium and they burned her at the stake! The "Letters of Paul" in the Bible speak of people having the "gift" and "speaking in voices." Of course the greatest medium of all was Jesus Christ who healed the sick, practised "absent healing" and was in constant communication with the next world. Spiritualists believe in nothing that can't be proved and our Spiritualist pioneers wanted evidence of the next world. They sought for and found their loved ones who wanted to make contact with them but were prevented from doing this by the established church who claimed you faced damnation if you drew aside the veil. The means to communicate with the next world have always existed and Christian churches who have tried to stop this communication have done a great wrong and could have saved many people from the fear of dying. Those who have passed to the next world have found out the truth for themselves — that life is eternal and that there are no "dead." The task of a medium is to provide evidence that life continues in the next world. He or she will bring to you the comfort that your loved one is still very much alive and aware of what is going on in your life. Many people criticize messages from mediums because of the trivial content of the messages but it is these so-called trivialities that provide such outstanding evidence that our loved ones are still around. Mediums will NOT give you messages about future events. That is fortune telling. Sadly many people who go to the special Evenings of Clairvoyance which are held by the churches are only there hoping for a message to tell them they will win the Lottery! They have no conception of the religious significance of Spiritualism and look for advice on their love affairs, financial problems etc. The medium is a channel to be used by those in the next world and can only give out to the audience what is being received just as a radio or TV set is switched on and tuned to a certain frequency. He or she will relay memories from loved ones that only the recipient can accept. It should be remembered that people in the next world do not become filled with wisdom on passing over. In the early years of the movement physical manifestations were necessary to convince unbelievers of survival after death. Today the concentration is on giving out messages from deceased relatives. We can communicate with our loved ones who are already in the next world waiting for us, we can receive teachings from evolved souls called Masters who are much higher up the ladder. Many such teachings, given to mediums have been published in book form thus making them available to a world-wide audience. In order to listen to more intelligent communications from the next world it is necessary to read the books of Silver Birch, Ramadan, and White Eagle to name but a few. Sometimes these "Masters" can entrance a medium's physical body and speak directly to the congregation and it is a very wonderful experience to listen to an inhabitant of the next world.

So — Spiritualism is a Religion, a Science but it is also a CODE OF CONDUCT for life. Of course all religions should be a way of life to their followers but many people are not prepared to carry their beliefs into everyday life. Because Spiritualists know that this earth life is only one step in a long, long journey through eternity and because we know that our progress on that journey depends on how we conduct ourselves here and now on this earth plane then we are inspired to do our best in whatever circumstances we find ourselves. We believe in "Cause and Effect," "Reaping and Sowing," "Compensation and Retribution." We believe that one day we will all have to answer for the life we have led on the earth. We do not believe that someone else "died for our sins". We believe that we must take personal responsibility for the life we are leading and, knowing that we must one day account for every thought, word and action does tend to keep one on the straight and narrow! As Spiritualists we believe in the importance of living a good life. We have the desire to

8

serve. We are aware of our duty to our God, our neighbour and our world. Spiritualism is a religion which gives meaning to life by teaching that we are not here by accident and that there was a reason why we were born into the world.

So — to sum up, Spiritualism is three things. It is a RELIGION which believes in God the creator of all life. It is a SCIENCE because it can prove the existence of the world we all go to when our time in this world is finished and it is a CODE OF CONDUCT by which we try to live a life that we will not be ashamed of when we review it in the world to come.

CHAPTER 2
WHAT I BELIEVE ABOUT GOD.

I believe in God. I believe in God with every ounce of my being — He is my heavenly Father, my friend, my counsellor and my guide. I talk to Him constantly. I confide in Him. I ask Him to help me through the difficult periods of my life. I thank Him for His goodness and I share with Him the simple joys and pleasures which I experience every day. I hope that statement will put an end to the erroneous belief which still abounds today that Spiritualists are in league with the devil! Spiritualism does not have a set of beliefs and creeds like other religious denominations but we do have what are called our "Seven Principles" which are accepted by all Spiritualists with some liberty of interpretation and the very first Principle of all is "The Fatherhood of God." Spiritualists believe that God is the Father of all peoples on the earth — not just of one race, not just of one nation and certainly not just of one religion! We believe that there is only one God for all and believing this makes us all members of one huge family.

I believe that God is the creator of the universe and of every single living thing that makes up that universe. I believe He is the Father of all humankind and not only of humans but of all living creatures who share this planet earth with us. Anyone who really studies the world of nature, the animal and bird kingdoms, the planet on which we all live, the vast universe of stars, must be aware that one mind holds everything together. One mind which has created life in all its forms from the tiniest flower to the largest mammal. The whole world runs according to the Law of Nature which is just another name for the Law of God. We break God's Law at our peril and the consequences fall on all of us. This is God's world and we would do well to remember this fact and think before we pollute it and destroy the creatures and other life forms who share this world with us.

Years ago people believed in a great many different gods. After a while they believed that every country had its own god. I believe there is only one God for the whole world, for each and every member of the human race. It has been said that God is too big for just one religion. Perhaps we call Him by different names and approach Him along different pathways but we are all going in the same direction. "There are many paths to reach the top of the mountain." Different religions follow different paths to God and all should be respected. "All roads lead to God." I do not believe that there is only one way to God. I do not believe that Christians have the right way, neither do I believe that any other sect or religion can make that claim. There is not a Roman Catholic God and a Protestant one! He is not just the God of the Christians be they Catholic, Protestant, Quaker, Methodist, Baptist and all the other Christian sects. He is also the God of the Jews, the Muslims, the Hindus and numerous other faiths and He is the God of the Agnostic, the Humanist and the Atheist. The Sikhs say that God is not interested in religious labels and Isaiah 45:5 tells us that there is one God for all.

The idea of a god "above the bright blue sky" and sitting on a throne was all right for the minds of primitive and undeveloped people but, modern man who knows all about space travel, is not going to accept this at all. Didn't one of the Russian astronauts say that he never saw God while he was out there! There is a world of difference between the God which the churches preach about and the Father of the Universe. They are leagues apart. God is not just the God of the Jews and to say that He preferred Israel to other countries is foolish. Two thousand years ago the Hebrew people were the only nation and race who came even close to knowing God but even they had it woefully wrong. They thought of Him as a vengeful deity who had to be constantly appeased by sacrifices. They ignored their own prophets who told them differently. "I desire mercy not sacrifice." [Hosea 6:6] "What doth the Lord require of thee but to do justly, and to love mercy and to walk humbly with thy God." [Micah 6:8]. God sent Jesus to the Jews to set them right but alas they were too stuck in their ways to make the changes. Those who did decide to accept the teachings of Jesus were called Christians but it should be remembered that Jesus was born a Jew, lived his whole life as a Jew and died as a member of the Jewish race. Jesus was never a Christian! It was St Paul and his followers around whom the name "Christian" evolved. I find it upsetting in today's world that churches seem to be putting the worship of Jesus above that of God. Spiritualists do not believe that Jesus was god. We believe that he was a messenger from God and it is God we are supposed to be worshipping — not Jesus! Buddhism was founded by Buddha but Buddhists do not worship him as a god. Buddhists are taught to look within themselves for answers and Jesus said something similar when he said that the Kingdom of God was within you. The Dalai Lama has said that there is no need for temples and complicated philosophy. Our own brain and heart is our Temple and the philosophy is kindness.

11

Every individual is a creation of God and He created us all as equals. No one religion is correct and every person on the earth belongs to God. The second principle of Spiritualism is "The Brotherhood of Man." If God is the Father of us all then it follows that all people in the world are members of one spiritual family — brothers and sisters all. Some of us are clothed in a white skin, others in a black skin and then there are all the shades in between. God liked variety in His big family! It matters not the colour of the skin, the race or the nationality, the different names given to God by the different churches, the faith or lack of faith of the individual, each and every member of the human race is a child of God and nothing can alter that fact. All humans have a responsibility for everything and everybody with whom they share their lives on this earth for we are all spiritual kith and kin. This principle was clearly demonstrated by Jesus when, in answer to the question, "Who is my neighbour?" he told the story of the Good Samaritan which shows quite clearly that all men (and women) are to be treated the same and not differently because of their nationality, class, colour or creed. As earthly parents pass on their genes to their offspring so God the creator of all life has given each one of us a portion of Himself. Each of us possesses a spark of the divine spirit of God. We are forever part of God as He is forever part of us. We are linked to Him by a sort of invisible thread and He will NEVER cut that thread. "Whither shall I flee from thy presence?" [Psalm 139:7] We do not need any man or supernatural being to bring us into the presence of God.

Perhaps I am lucky in that I have been conscious of the presence of God all of my life. However the way I was taught about religion made me afraid of Him! I was given the idea that God would punish me for my childish wrongs. I thought of Him as a stern headmaster just waiting to pounce on me! "Thou God seest me" as the Victorian bedroom texts put it. Now Jesus I could love! He was the friend of little children. It was not until years later when I took up Bible study in earnest that I stopped being afraid of God. Jesus said "look at me and see what God is like." [John 14:9] He spoke of the shepherd looking for the lost sheep, the fact that not a sparrow died but God was aware of it and he likened God to the father of the prodigal son. In fact, Jesus told the people of his day over and over again that God loved them so why is that over 2000 years later the message has still not got through? The answer is orthodox religion with its insistence on the performance of certain rituals and the necessity of believing certain things in order to be accepted by God. God is a loving faithful father and not a vengeful deity. Many earthly fathers are kind and forgiving and surely God cannot be worse than His own creation? Spiritualism preaches of a loving God who loves even the lowest of His creation. We do not recognise a God who required a human sacrifice as appeasement for sin. We do not recognise a God who punishes sinners and sends them to an everlasting torture in Hell. We do not believe that certain people have been "Elected" to go to heaven. We believe in a God who is perfect, pure, loving and holy and who is absolutely incapable of tyranny, cruelty and human vices. We believe in a God who so loves each and everyone of us that He wants us to grow into perfect beings and He will go on waiting for us to reach that standard no matter how long it takes. He will never cease to love us but we believe that all our wrong deeds must be put right before any advancement is possible. We believe that everyone must work at their own salvation and not become purified by simply accepting certain beliefs. Another one of our seven principles is "Personal Responsibility" and I like that! I am the master of my fate, I am the captain of my soul. ["Invictus" by W.E. Henley.] I will climb the ladder to heaven by my own efforts. "Show me the stairway that I have to climb" as a modern hymn puts it but the hand of God is always there to help me along the way. No soul will ever be lost but nobody saves you but yourself.

What about people who don't believe in God at all? Many Agnostics, Atheists and Humanists deny the existence of God and yet live a good life and work for the good of their fellow men. In fact these people may be closer to God's message of love than those who claim to be religious. They will be very surprised to find themselves in the next world when they leave this one. They will then realize that they were doing the will of God all the time even if they never knew it! Remember that because you don't believe in God it does not mean that He does not exist! The most famous of all our spirit guides from the next world is called Silver Birch and he tells us that God (whom he always refers to as the Great Spirit) is not worried whether a person believes in Him or not. God knows all about you. Even the hairs of your head are counted! He is not going to cast you off just because you have not yet found Him. At this point a regular churchgoer might protest — what advantage do I have because of my faith in God? The advantage that believers have over non-believers is that believers can enjoy the presence, comfort and friendship of God in this world while unbelievers must struggle through life on their own. John Buchan has described an atheist as "a man with no invisible means of support." Dr William Barclay in one of his books has said that the tragedy of life is that so many people are trying to live their life without contact with the invisible world and with God. Many people cannot face up to the trials of life and declare that they have lost their faith in God. "If God is a God of Love why did He let this happen to me?" We live in an age of nervous breakdowns, suicides, especially among the young, divorce, physical and mental abuse, drug taking. We hear of people getting counselling. How did people cope with problems before the age of counselling? I think in many ways the human race has gone soft. The reason for this is that we have lost contact with God who is our strength. Many of our troubles in life come from the fact that we try to do things ourselves when we ought to ask God for help. If we put God in the centre of our lives then we cannot go far wrong. As Jesus put it "Seek ye first the Kingdom of God and His righteousness and all these things shall be added unto you." [Matthew 6:33] I never make a decision without asking God's advice and the answer always comes. You will be surprised how quickly the answer comes. Believers have a friend to turn to in time of trouble, someone to talk to when there is no one else to listen, someone to ask for guidance and help in time of need. Someone to help us over the hurdles of life, through the dark rivers of despair and we have the knowledge that only a faith in God can give us when we face death or bereavement. The unbeliever has to bear all these problems alone. However believers in God do not live lives free from suffering — otherwise everyone would be flocking to join up! Spiritualists believe that our life is a testing ground for the soul. (More about this in a later chapter.) You are living a life today because God gave it to you for a purpose.

I believe in God! He is more real to me than any other person on earth. I can talk to Him about anything. He knows all about my life and what makes me tick. He is a God for the 21st Century who understands computers! After all He caused them to be discovered and invented! He is not a God of 2000 years ago, He is a God of the here and now and He longs to be of help to His creation. Until the churches put this idea across they will continue to lose members. Religion must be seen to work! People want a modern God who understands their problems. Well, He does understand your problems! He is the greatest counsellor of them all. He knows the solution to your problems, what is best for you and He cannot fail for HE IS GOD!

CHAPTER 3
WHAT I BELIEVE ABOUT JESUS.

I believe that Jesus Christ was the most perfect person to have ever been born into this world. Spiritualists believe that Jesus was the first soul to reach the pinnacle of soul perfection and ascend to the highest rung of Heaven. All our spirit guides agree on this. As such he is closest in character and nature to God. Spiritualists do not believe that he was the ONLY son of God because we believe that we are all sons and daughters of God who is our heavenly Father. Did not Jesus himself teach us to say "Our Father" and he spoke of Him as "My Father and your Father." Perhaps there is a sense in which we could describe him as the "first-born son of God" because he was the first to reach the top! However he did say that what he did we could do also. Jesus gave up his glory in the next world to return to the earth and spread the word of what God is really like and how He wants us to behave. He came to show us the way to God. He said over and over again "I am the way" [John 14:6] and the earliest followers of Jesus called themselves followers of the WAY. Jesus tried in his short ministry (33 years) to show people a different God — a God who loved, who forgave, who understood and who longed to be known to His people. Jesus tried to put his message across by using simple everyday stories (Parables). He told of the shepherd seeking the lost sheep and not giving up until he had it safely in the fold with the others. Here he was trying to tell them that no matter how far anyone strayed from the path of righteousness, God would seek until He found them and bring them into His kingdom. In other words no one will ever be "lost." To show God's forgiveness of sinners he recounted the story of the Prodigal Son who, after leading a dissipated life was welcomed home by a joyful and forgiving father. Jesus said that his own life was a living personification of God. "He who hath seen me hath seen the Father." [John14:9] One of our spirit guides from the next world (White Eagle) has said "Humanity has been shown the most perfect manifestation in Christ of the highest ideal of God in man." Over the centuries there have been human instruments who have been used as teachers to bring knowledge and Jesus is the greatest of these.

Jesus was the loveliest person who ever walked the earth. Everyone loved him (except the church representatives). He was invited to weddings and parties where he was the guest of honour. If this is what God is like what do we have to fear? Jesus came as an ambassador for God. The job of an ambassador is to represent his country and his monarch so Jesus came as God's representative. Spiritualists do not believe that Jesus himself is a god. He himself said in Matthew 4:10 that it is to God alone that we must direct our worship. It seems to me that the church today almost leaves God out of their worship. It is all Jesus, Jesus. Jesus! The Bible clearly tells us that we must worship God and "Him only shalt thou serve." [Matt. 4:10] Jesus was born into the Jewish race. He lived all his life as a Jew (indeed he is often referred to in the Bible as Rabbi) and he died as a Jew. When he was 12 years old he was taken to Jerusalem and he became lost in the temple to the distress of his parents. Well he was there to take his Bar-Mizvah which all Jewish boys take at about the age of 12. When he died he was still a Jew — he was never a Christian and many people today seem to be unaware of this fact. The name "Christian" was given to his followers and remember that everyone of his original followers — Peter, Andrew, Paul etc were also Jews. I find it incredible that discrimination still exists against the Jewish race when the loveliest person the world has ever known had that nationality. The mother of Jesus was a Jewish maiden and would never have been a golden haired madonna! Jesus himself would have had an olive skin and dark hair as would all the disciples and the earliest followers of Jesus. A communicant from the next world spoke of seeing Jesus for the first time but not recognising him as she had always been taught that he had a white skin and fair hair! Out of all today's religions, Christianity should be closest to the Jewish faith as it is simply an offshoot of Judaism. It has been said that Jesus came to prepare a kingdom for God and his followers went off and founded another church! Jesus condemned the church of his day because of its stupid rules and regulations which made religion an intolerable burden on the people. The religious authorities of the day hated Jesus and never forgave him. He dared to tell them that their ideas about the Sabbath were all wrong. "The Sabbath was made for man, and not man for the Sabbath." [Mark 2:27] To the Jews the Sabbath was not a day of rest and enjoyment. It was a day of fear when so many things were forbidden, for the church loved its rules more than it loved human beings. It was considered a sin for a woman to wear a brooch on her dress on the Sabbath because that would be "carrying a burden!" The religious authorities of his time put fear into the hearts of their people by preaching of a God who needed pacifying with constant altar sacrifices. The Temple at Jerusalem ran red with the blood of innocent animals sacrificed in this senseless way. The Prophets of old had again and again told the people of Israel that God did not require such sacrifices. Jesus was shocked at the corruption being practised in the Temple whereby poor people were being swindled by being told that their sacrifice was not good enough and forcing them to buy one from the local stalls at a much higher price. We hear a lot about a "gentle Jesus" but remember that Jesus was all human as well as godly and this human side of his nature erupted into a righteous anger when he took a whip and drove the money lenders from the Temple while overturning their stalls. No doubt this enjoyable event witnessed by the worshippers was spoken about for years to come!

Into the Jewish religion which was tied down by rules and rituals he came like a breath of fresh air. People however are very set in their ways and the religious authorities were aghast at what he was saying and preaching. Despite the wonderful cures he did of disease and illness they did everything in their power to discredit him. If Jesus came back to the earth today and told our Church authorities that they had got it all wrong I wonder what their reaction would be? People like to carry on in the same little rut they are used to. They do not want to be jolted out of a comfortable routine. Richard Holloway (a former Bishop of Edinburgh) has said that the church spends too much time burnishing the remembrance of Jesus and not enough in following his example of living. This is how it was in Israel 2000 years ago. The priests of the day saw Jesus as a rebel against their code of practices. If he was allowed to continue this preaching goodness only knows what would happen. He had to be got rid of. They tried to trap him every way they could. The woman taken in adultery is a classic example. The Law of Moses said that such people should meet death by stoning. They confronted Jesus with the woman and asked his opinion. If Jesus had said "obey the Law" he would be shown to go against his own preaching of a merciful and loving God. If he said "free her" he would be breaking the religious law. His reply is a masterpiece of diplomacy —"Let he who is without sin cast the first stone." [John 8:7] Now, nobody in that mob 2000 years ago could claim to be sinless and so the woman's life was saved. "Go and sin no more" Jesus told her — like God who gives us more than one chance to live a good life. In the end his enemies had to bribe one of his followers to betray him. In a trumped up charge, in a travesty of a trial he was quickly condemned to the death sentence of the day.

Did Jesus really die on the cross? I have recently read a book which has made me doubt this fact — "The Jesus Conspiracy" by Holger Kersten. The book bases its findings on the fact that the shroud in which the body of Jesus was supposedly wrapped shows, by the bloodstains on it, that the body was still bleeding when it was taken down from the cross and — corpses don't bleed! The writer tells a wonderful story in which the disciples had a plan to rescue Jesus. He was drugged on the cross, taken to an already prepared nearby tomb where he was revived and smuggled away to the Essene community. What a wonderful Hollywood movie this would make! Does this alter my belief in God and in the preaching of Jesus? Not a bit! If Jesus managed to outwit his enemies and live to a ripe old age I think it is just great! I do not doubt for one minute the real life and existence of Jesus but I think that so many old pagan legends have become attached to his life that the real Jesus has been obscured. Historical books, quite apart from the Bible, verify the existence of Jesus and describe him as a travelling Rabbi of the Galilee region who met with a cruel and untimely death at the hands of the Romans. Jesus himself never gave the slightest hint that he intended to die for humanity. In fact in the Garden of Gethsamene he is said to have begged God to take "this cup" away from him. The idea of a resurrected Jesus dying for our sins came from St Paul and the story of the empty tomb is much older than the story of the resurrection. Our spirit guides in the next world often refer to Jesus whom they call the Nazarene. They tell us he is still working from the next world on behalf of mankind. Someone once asked Silver Birch "Did Jesus really die on the cross?" The answer given was "the manner of his death is unimportant, it is his life you should be trying to emulate." What a wonderful reply and what a diplomatic answer! Think of the uproar that would ensue if it was ever proved that Jesus did not die on the cross! The whole Christian religion is based on the idea that Jesus sacrificed his life for your sins thus taking away from you all responsibility for your actions. This is the exact opposite of the Spiritualist religion which says that we are responsible for our own actions and therefore for our own salvation. When someone famous dies we do not remember them because of HOW they died but because of how they lived. Except for immediate family and friends many of us will forget what our famous entertainers died of but we will always remember the laughter they brought into our lives, their wonderful singing voices and the happiness they gave us. I don't know how or when Sir Alexander Fleming died but I remember that he saved many lives because of his discovery of penicillin. The same can be said of all great scientists, inventors, discoverers and others who made our world a better place to live in. Jesus should be remembered for his teachings about God and not for the death penalty which he suffered at the hands of his enemies. Calvary was the work of man not of God. God did not want Jesus to die when his work was only just beginning. The church would have us worship the man but forget his message. They are so busy adoring and praising Jesus that they forget his teachings. Jesus does not want all this adoration and praise from the churches. He wants them to carry on his teachings, free men's souls and make them realize the truth about God. However the world does not like to be told unwelcome truths. If Jesus came back into the world today and denounced our ceremonial religion would he fare any better than 2000 years ago? His rules of conduct for life are far too spiritual to suit an age which wants luxury and ease. His teachings are too piercing to be popular. In many ways the world is still not ready to receive the advanced truths which he taught. Jesus was a religious revolutionary, the "Rebel with a cause" for his age and he was also the "angry young man" of his day.

What Jesus did for Judaism, Spiritualism tries to do for Christianity. We don't want to do away with the wonderful teachings which Jesus brought to the earth but we do want to show the true spiritual meaning of those teachings. The Bible speaks of "sowing and reaping" [Gal 6:7] and Spiritualism teaches about the Law of Cause and Effect. The mission of Jesus when he came to this earth was to do away with Jewish rituals and with petty rules and regulations which had absolutely nothing to do with living your life according to God's laws. "Ye shall know the truth" [John 8:32] he said and tried to show them all, that the way of God was for the improvement of humanity. He told men that God wanted them to be merciful, truthful, pure, honest, self-denying and repentant for sins committed and he was a living example of the life he preached. He taught a duty to God as well as to your fellow man. He inspired all who heard him. The teachings of Jesus are the only teachings that anyone needs. Spiritualists follow the same truths that Jesus taught and we believe in the "do's and don'ts" which he spoke about. We speak of man's progressive destiny and of God's unceasing love and out Spirit Guides tell us that in the next world they work under the direction of Jesus to further these truths on the earth.

David Livingstone said about Jesus "He is a gentleman whose word can be trusted" and I would certainly go along with that.

19

CHAPTER 4
WHAT I BELIEVE IS THE PURPOSE OF LIFE.

The majority of people on this earth have absolutely no idea why they are here so one of the aims of Spiritualism is to explain the purpose and reason for your existence. If everyone understands this then surely it will make them really look at their lives, take stock and consider the effect of their actions on those around them. Many people live their lives without once thinking of the implications of their actions. Human beings can cause many problems by behaving in a selfish manner, by causing a life time of heartache to someone by uttering cruel words, by holding someone back in their development. They do not assist others but live solely for themselves. Magnus, the guide of the medium Colin Fry, has said that the human spirit needs to start thinking of "we" and not "I." When the time comes for them to leave this world and see a review of their life in the next world they will have problems! One of the seven Principles of Spiritualism is "Personal Responsibility." So — you are the one responsible for your own life and you make the bed you will have to lie on. You have free will, you make your own choices.

One of our spirit teachers from the next world is called Ramadan and he has compared us all to little ships setting sail upon the sea of life. Before we arrive in this world we have already chosen our course. Many of us would like to rest in some safe little harbour, sheltered from the storms of life but we are meant to launch out onto the great river of life and become enriched by all we see and experience. You will not learn anything if you don't try to experience as much as you can in your life. Every happening in your life is an opportunity. Every corner you go round, every fence you jump over, every boulder you manage to push out of the way all contribute to your spiritual growth. The Rodgers and Hammerstein song "Climb Every Mountain" expresses this sentiment beautifully. Everyone is responsible for their own progress and it is up to us all to use our time on the earth wisely. No one is perfect. Failing is part of trying and if you don't try then you can't fail. Don't dwell on regrets (mistakes are lessons to be learned). Try to let go of your bad experiences and build on your achievements. It is the way you face your problems that builds your character.

Do we decide on the life we must lead before we are born into this world? Well I do believe that with the help of spirit advisers we choose the life we need to further our destiny. I believe we choose our parents and the place on earth where we will be born. I think we are all shown a plan for our life before we are born but sadly we cannot remember that plan and, with our gift of free will, there is no one around to force us to stay on the chosen path. Spirit guides may try to help us but nobody can drive us along a particular road. At the end of our life, with the help of these same advisers, we will review our life and see what progress we have made. We will never learn anything unless we face up to the consequences of our actions. Nothing terrible will happen to us if we do not follow our chosen plan but how sad that at the end of our earthly existence we will look back and see how we lost the way and missed out on golden opportunities. In fact we may beg those in the next world to let us go back and try again but how many "shots" at life must we have before we get it right and progress along our spiritual path? Years ago when studying for exams I had many fellow students who had taken the course and the exams quite a few times. The reason that they kept failing was that they only put in a half-effort to master the subject instead of going all out to learn and pass it at the first attempt. They wasted their time and held back on their own career prospects. We should all try our best not to fail in the "exams of life."

I do not propose to discuss reincarnation in this book. It is a subject that is widely disagreed upon not only in this world but, strangely, also in the next! I myself believe in reincarnation because it makes sense to me. How can we learn everything in one life? If you are born to middle class parents in comfortable circumstances how do you know what it is like to be born to poverty stricken parents. If you are born healthy how do you know what it is like to be born disabled? If you are born with intelligence how do you know what it is like to have learning difficulties. The list of what might have been in your life is endless. If we do come back to have another go at life then I think we will come back to a different sex, race or skin colour and I think it will be to completely different circumstances from the previous time around. However I have no wish to know about any previous lives I may have led. A Spirit Guide has said that even if reincarnation is true it is unimportant and that you could spend so much time looking over your shoulder into the past that you would lose the chance to be efficient in the present. I believe that we will have chosen our new life because it will help our soul to grow. The spirit world speaks of our soul as being like a diamond with different facets. In order to see the true beauty of the diamond it is necessary that each facet is polished to perfection. That is one explanation of the concept of reincarnation. If you believe in Karma then you may believe that you have to continually return to the earth to expunge the sins of a previous existence. I have heard though that you can work off your sins by service in the next world. One thing I have prayed all my life is that when I reach the next world I will be allowed to stay there for ever! I prayed this prayer when I was a very small child and I am sure that at that stage of my life I had never even heard of the word "reincarnation." I think I was born knowing about successive lives and I have always felt that I was an "old soul."

Everyone's life is a collection of both pleasant and unpleasant experiences. We need both in our life because if you have never been unhappy how do you know what happiness is? These days many people blame their misfortunes in life on an unhappy, deprived childhood. "I never had a chance." We read of young criminals getting "background" reports before they are sentenced. Years ago thousands of people suffered deprived childhoods but they did not go on to become criminals. My own mother was one of a large family where visits to the pawn shop were a weekly occurrence. One of her brothers entered the Merchant Navy, another worked for the Prison Service, her sisters married and increased their standard of living and their children went on to study at colleges and universities. I am sure many of that generation could say the same. You are what you make of yourself. How you deal with misfortune is what shapes your character. Adversity is a test of the soul and you must overcome adversity. Don't blame God because you fail to take advantage of the opportunities which life offers you.

Throughout your life God provides these opportunities, gives you the means and the tools for you to fulfil your purpose in life. It does not matter what your path in life is, as long as you live honestly, try your best and also use all the gifts and talents that God has given you. Everyone is born with a talent or gift of some sort and if you don't use the ability and brains that God gave you then you are cheating God and yourself. Your gifts were given to you, so freely give them out to the world. It is by using your gifts for the betterment of the world that your soul will progress. The Rev William Barclay has said that any gift that a man (or woman) has, must be placed ungrudgingly at the service of the community. As believers in God we must realise that everything we have (be it material possessions or talents) must be used in God's service and that means in the service of our fellow men. Many people take and take from the world and seldom think of putting something back in. Maybe we can't all do great things but we can do the small things of life in a great way. We can all be very useful little cogs in the big wheel of life. The essence of life is to work and use those talents we have and if we do not use them then we will lose them. Remember what Jesus taught in the parable of the talents.[Matthew 25:15-30]. Nowadays many people seem to have lost their sense of direction in life. Perhaps the "nanny state" we hear about is responsible for this. People no longer believe in saving for their old age "let the state keep me!" Charles W. Colson has said "The loss of meaning, purpose and individual dignity is the growing malaise of our times." We have beggars on the streets, most of them young healthy adults who say they cannot find employment. When I see this I remember a young school leaver who wrote to my place of employment and offered to work for us for 2 days a week for nothing in order to gain the experience. Impressed by this we took her on. Some months later she was put on the payroll as a part-timer and eventually we gave her full-time employment. Today she holds a qualified post in her chosen career. Indeed, God helps those who help themselves.

You cannot live the life of others for them no matter how close to them you are and you have to remember that every soul is at a different stage of development. We are all climbing a ladder and we are all on different rungs. You can climb to the highest or fall to the lowest it is your choice. Perhaps some of us are born to a greater destiny than others but I believe that we have all been born to fulfil some purpose. You may consider yourself to be a very insignificant person but you are still someone that God can use for his purposes. A medium said to me once "God does not want your ability — He wants your availability." You should try to so live your life that the earth is enriched by your presence. "The purpose or function in life is to contribute in a positive way to the world in which we live" (the words of DATA in Star Trek -TNG). Life is not easy but it is not meant to be easy! Every step forward in life has to be earned by hard work, discipline and self-sacrifice. If believing in God gave us all automatic security against the trials and tribulations of life wouldn't everyone be queuing up to join a church? Remember that the Bible tells us that God sends the rain on the just as well as the unjust. Remember also that Jesus was the most righteous person who ever lived and look what happened to him! Oh no, life is not easy but you have within you the strength to overcome all of life's trials. One of my favourite verses from the Bible is "I will be with you when you pass through the waters" [Isaiah 43:2] and, when I have faced some crisis in my life, I have only got through it by holding on tightly to the hand of God.

One of the main obstacles to our spiritual progress is that we attach too much importance to trivial things. I heard a talk years ago by the then Chief Constable of Grampian Police. He said that there were only three things we needed in life to survive — shelter, food and clothes and he said that he would add a fourth one of a hope or goal to strive for. We have got our priorities all wrong. I remember having an argument once with a colleague who claimed that a television was a necessity of life while I said that it was a luxury. Now, I appreciate my television (and my video) but in no way are they necessary to my life and in fact I know people who live quite happily without either. We desire possessions, riches, power and we think more about these things than we do about the destiny of our soul. Our Spirit Guides tell us that the greatest obstacle to our spiritual development is our love of material things. When we leave this world we have to leave all our possessions behind us. "There are no pockets in a shroud." We only carry into the next world the characters we have formed. Again Jesus had a word to say about this when he spoke of storing up treasure which would not rust.[Matthew 6:19-21] What would be the point of getting an education and acquiring knowledge if we could not take it all with us when the time comes for us to leave the earth?

Do not envy others their possessions and their talents but do the best you can with the ones that you possess. Don't think that you are no use to anyone because God put you in the place you are for a special reason and He has something that you and only you can do for Him. I read once that each of us are necessary in this world for perhaps just one moment in time when we are the only ones available to do a certain thing. I have always prayed that I would not fail Him in my chosen moment. Don't look for rewards in this world. It is at the end of your earthly life that you will reap the benefits and get what you earned and what you deserve. None of us should waste our earthly years. We should view them as a preparation for our new life which begins at death.

The person who has loved God and his fellow men, who has honestly tried to live a good life, worked hard at the chosen occupation, endeavoured to improve himself and helped others in their life, this is the soul which makes progress. The soul that is selfish, self-indulgent, lazy, refuses to learn and better himself is the soul that makes no progress and will have to return to earth to take the exams of life again. We all need a code of behaviour to follow and this is where the Ten Commandments and the teachings of Jesus come in. The art of life is to do the best you can with the resources you have. Fate is what life gives you but destiny is what you make of it. You should constantly ask God what He wants you to do with your life. Do nothing that you would be ashamed of because remember your every action and every spoken word are known and recorded in the Rolls of Remembrance. We live in an immoral age when purity is laughed at and we all want to fit in with the crowd but someone has said that civilization may stink but we don't have to smell of it!

Each of you is a unique individual and very important to God. We all chose to be born on the earth. We all want to be needed. Well — God needs you! When someone has come close to death they often say "God saved my life for a purpose." Well I believe we are all here for a purpose. Have you found your purpose in life?

CHAPTER 5
WHAT I BELIEVE ABOUT DEATH.

"Men fear death as children fear to go in the dark." That is a quotation from an essay by Francis Bacon which I learned while at school. It is something that I have never forgotten. Children grow out of their fear of the dark. Why is it that people do not grow out of their fear of death? Every single person who is born into this world is one day going to leave it. As the Bible book of Ecclesiastes puts it [Ecc. 3:2] "There is a time to be born and a time to die." When you are required to go into the next world nothing and nobody can halt that journey. I think that the reason that people are afraid to die is that they don't know what awaits them. There is still appalling ignorance about what happens following physical death. If you really believe that death is the end then you will think that life is futile. Why bother if you are not going to survive. Why study? Why take the exam? Eat, drink and be merry etc!

Most people go through life never giving much thought to what happens next and it is only after they experience the loss of a loved one that they start to wonder about the afterlife. Shakespeare (in Hamlet) has called it "the undiscovered country from whose bourn no traveller returns." However Shakespeare did not know about Spiritualism! In a Spiritualist Church these travellers do return to reassure us that they are still very much alive and to tell us a bit of what it is like where they are living. Other churches offer sympathy at a time of death but that is all. They will speak of faith in a life after death (but they never tell us about it) and that does not really help a mourner. Ordinary people these days have no religion and less and less people are going to church. The bereaved want more than sympathy. They want to know what has happened to their loved ones, where have they gone to and will they ever see them again. They require proof and that is where Spiritualism can help. Proving survival after death is at the heart of Spiritualist teaching. Millions of people are desperate to know that life does not end for them in this world and Spiritualist Churches must do more to spread this knowledge and get the message across. Spiritualism believes that we should all have this knowledge while on earth for then we are better prepared for what awaits us. We speak these days of knowing the "facts of life." Well, everyone should know the "facts of death" as well. We should all know where we came from, why we came and where we are going to. After all if you were considering emigrating to another country you would want to find out as much as you could about it before you set off for your new life.

Too many people today run away from the idea of death. They follow special diets and exercise regimes in an effort to prolong their lives. Seneca has said that "men do not care how nobly they live but only how long." Our medical profession is obsessed with the idea of replacing parts of our anatomy to allow us to live longer. The motive may be good for a young life but is it good for one of more advanced years? Many elderly people, whose body has outlived its usefulness, start to look forward to being re-united with loved ones and long to be free of a body which no longer obeys their wishes. Indeed many beg not to be resuscitated. They yearn to be free and death is the gift that gives them that freedom. We must all learn to accept the fact that death is the next stage of our existence because we cannot die — we are all immortal. Death is not the end but a gate we pass through on our way to a continuance of life into the next world. Life is a journey. Earth is not your permanent home. It is like a bridge you are walking across and you are not meant to stay on that bridge forever.

Death to me is like falling asleep and indeed this phrase is often used on gravestones and in burial records. Nobody is afraid of falling asleep and indeed if you are very very tired you long for sleep to overcome you. I don't fear death — only perhaps the run up to death because nobody wants a painful end to their earthly existence. I am not afraid to die and I don't believe that I will die one minute before God wants me to enter the next world. What happens at the moment of death? Does it hurt? When the physical body can no longer function it separates from the spiritual body. The two bodies are held together by a Silver Cord (which is referred to in the Bible — Ecc. 12:6) in exactly the same way as the umbilical cord unites mother and child. When that cord is severed the child begins a separate existence and exactly the same thing happens at death. The spirit with the soul is gently withdrawn from the body and what is left is just the empty shell. Spirit people refer to this as your "envelope." People have been known to say when looking at a dead body "but he/she is not there!" They are aware that the vital living force has withdrawn. We all speak of people "leaving this earth", "passing on" or "what a nice way to go." Such phrases have become part of our language so deep inside of all of us is the knowledge that death is just a leaving and a passing and not an ending. Silver Birch is one of our most famous guides from the next world, and he has compared death to the freeing from the cage of the imprisoned bird. What a wonderful image that conjures up. When you die you leave behind you all your aches, pains and physical defects. Once freed from the physical frame you will be completely whole in mind and body. William Roache (Ken Barlow in Coronation Street) although not a Spiritualist is interested in the movement and he wrote an article for our "Two Worlds" magazine (April 2003) describing his search for the truth. In this article he calls death a change of environment — like walking out of a smoke-filled room into the fresh air.

These days we are fortunate in having about us many people who have had a "near death experience" or an N.D.E. as it is often referred to. These people have died albeit for just a few moments before they are drawn back into their bodies and they all tell a similar story. They are drawn towards a bright light, they are met by a loving, all-knowing being who shows them a review of their life, they see loved ones who have already passed over and then they are told to "go back because your time has not yet come." Such an event seems to leave a remarkable impression on those who have experienced it. They return to their lives with renewed determination to make something of themselves, to be better people and to live a life that they will not be ashamed to face up to when they again meet that "Being of Light" "Angel of Death" or whatever your religious faith would have you call it. Also they have completely lost their fear of dying. We have all heard the story of Lazarus whom Jesus called back from the grave. Legend has it that he remained a sad person to the end of his days because he had glimpsed paradise and was pulled back from it. Christians celebrate Easter Sunday as the day that Jesus rose from the dead but every day is a day when millions rise from the dead and enter the Gates of Heaven. All death leads to resurrection and onto a new life. Death must come before such a new life can begin. I have heard death compared to Winter when all nature appears to die only to burst into life again when Spring comes. Think of the seed which falls into the ground and "dies" in order to grow to a fuller life.

We in the west tend to think of death as the ultimate tragedy. In the east life is thought of as a continuous cycle of birth and death, the "Wheel of Life." The Spirit World does not see death as the tragedy that we do. Silver Birch has said "You cry when a soul comes to this world but we rejoice that a soul has come home." He has also said that we rejoice when a baby is born into our world but there are tears shed in the Spirit World because a loved one has left them to endure a life on the earth plane. Silver Birch teaches that the life we spend on earth is but a few seconds on the time scale of eternity. It is entirely wrong to believe that the God who gave you life, who has watched you grow from childhood to adulthood and beyond is just going to ditch you when death comes. What — and waste all that growing and learning you have done? Rudyard Kipling has put it this way in his poem "The Sack of the Gods." "He never wasted a leaf or a tree. Do you think He would squander souls?" You came from God and however long it takes you are going to work your way back to God.

I have been attending Spiritualist Churches since I was a teenager and I have heard many messages from the so-called dead and every message is about happiness on the other side with no wish to return to the earth. Perhaps I had better qualify that statement. Those who have led selfish, wicked lives will approach death with fear and they will not find happiness in the next world until they have come to terms with their wrongdoings and sought to make amends. There is nothing to fear about death if you have led a decent life. We cry when we lose a loved one in death but you know we are really crying for ourselves because we miss their physical presence. "Oh for the touch of a vanished hand and the sound of a voice that is still....." as the poet puts it (Break, Break, Break by Alfred Lord Tennyson). Excessive grief means you are mourning your own loss. Don't shed tears for those who have gone into the next world. They are much better off. Remember the final words of Sydney Carton in Charles Dickens "A Tale of Two Cities" — "it is a far, far better place I go to than I have ever been before." Lord Dowding was a very famous Spiritualist and he said that we should look forward to death as something to be desired when our life's work is done. Love is stronger than death and nothing can ever separate you from your loved ones. Of course we will always miss them but they want us to carry on with our own lives. They don't want us to sit and cry for ever. When I first experienced bereavement I asked someone how long it took to "get over it." She said to me "You don't get over it, you learn to live with it." I thought this was the most sensible thing that anyone had said to me at that time. No indeed you will never get over it. Your life has changed and will never be the same again so you have to learn to live a new life in a new way. We must try to be glad that they have gone to a better place and look forward to meeting them again when our time to cross over comes.

Making contact with a loved one in spirit will not end your grieving for only time can do that. It will however ease your anguish for you will know that they are "still there." I can remember when my mother died and I wanted desperately to know that she had safely reached "the other side" and was with my father. Oh the joy and relief of that first communication when I knew that they were both together in the next world. However once a mourner has received definite proof that their loved one is well and happy in the next world there is really no need for them to go on seeking for more and more communications. To hear from them from time to time is very nice but Spiritualism is not about dying it is about living! So live your life that your loved ones will be proud of you and when you eventually meet up with them they will say "Well Done." One of these recent TV programmes about mediums speaking to the dead featured a woman who had lost a loved one in an accident. She was going from medium to medium to hear from this person. She had already received ample proof that her loved one was all right in the next world but she could not leave it alone. She was told the person concerned had moved on since the accident and had a new life and that she must do the same. I thought if I was in the next world and kept getting constant messages that I was "wanted on the telephone" to communicate with the earth I would be a bit annoyed about it. We do not "rest in peace" in the next world but are all actively involved in work or study of some kind. Opponents of Spiritualism say that it is wrong to "raise the dead" as they call it but nobody in the next world is forced to come back and communicate. However if they truly love someone still on the earth and they see that loved one grieving for them then they will want to communicate and let them know that they are still there, feeling fine and still love them. One reason that so many of us want to get in touch with our loved ones in the next world is because we know that what has happened to them will one day happen to us. The communications which come through should forever take away our fear of dying and I have never yet heard a communicator express a wish to return to this world.

The aim of spiritualism is to dry the tears, provide solace to the bereaved, remove the fear of death and prove that life on earth is not the end of the road. Millions and millions of souls are arriving in the next world every day. They are bewildered, confused and dazed and it needs many workers in the next world to help them. People who are very ill and die in hospital will awaken in a hospital in the next world in order to minimize the shock to their spirit. I heard one spirit communicator describing her awakening in the next world. (This was from a Leslie Flint tape). She opened her eyes to a hospital ward and she felt very much better and decided that her new treatment must be working. One of the "Nurses" told her that she had a visitor. The visitor was her sister who had died some years previously. She looked at her sister and said "but you're dead!" and her sister replied "yes dear, and so are you!" There is really nothing to fear about going to the next world and the evidence for individual survival is overwhelming. A court of law would have to accept the evidence. Young children have foster mothers to care for them (perhaps related by blood) and pet animals are looked after by animal lovers until their masters or mistresses join them.

There are of course some people who very much desire to end their lives on this earth plane and they commit suicide. However death does not provide a way of escape from your problems because you cannot die! They have just given themselves the added problem of entering the next world before their appointed time and this results in spiritual confusion. Many religious people believe that if you commit suicide you go to Hell but this is not true. The soul is punished by seeing the effect of the suicide upon the loved ones left on earth. What happened to make them want to take their own life? It must have been a lack of love, understanding and help and they will certainly receive these things in their new life and they will be helped to understand the events that caused them to commit the act of suicide. It is really very sad because they have failed the tests or exams of life and may have to return to "resit" them. However some people take their own lives because they are in unbearable pain and of course this motive will be taken into consideration by those in the next world. I have every sympathy with those who are in such terrible pain or otherwise enduring a life of agony that they wish to take their own life. It should be remembered that it is not God who is keeping them alive in this anguish but the medical profession with their drugs. It is wrong to keep people alive by artificial means. If someone's time has come it is not kind to keep them alive without any hope of recovery. We are put on this earth to learn lessons and, if there is nothing left for a soul to learn in its lifetime, then its time has come to depart and the body cannot continue. When the time is right the spirit leaves the body and no machine can make it stay. No one should interfere in this process and others should not be given the responsibility of making that decision. What about Euthanasia? The spirit world does not agree with this as they say that the spirit is released before its time and also who takes responsibility for the act? However again motive is taken into consideration and such souls are met with love and understanding in the next world.

Then we have the problem of abortion which is at the other end of the scale. While the spirit world will accept contraception it says that abortion is wrong. They say it is akin to murder and while the act itself is condemned if it is for compassionate reasons then this will be taken into consideration. Everyone should realise however that the fertilised seed lives on in the next world. You may have destroyed the physical but you cannot destroy the spirit which is thrust rudely back into the next world where it will continue to grow and one day you will have to meet that aborted child whom you rejected. Still-born infants are cared for by foster mothers (who may be relatives) and they also grow to maturity in the next world. All these children have lost any earthly experience which would have helped their development but on the other hand they do not have to unlearn life's errors and make amends for sins committed.

What about ghosts? These are souls who just can't believe that they are dead because they are so obsessed with earthly things. They just do not realize that they have "died." Such people are often just confused and scared and to practise exorcism on them is wrong when what they need is love and help to cross over. They need the help of a medium to pass into the next world. The medium will send out thoughts to the next world and from there someone will come who will be known to the "ghost". It will be explained to them what has happened and they will be led away to start their new life. There are many workers in the spirit world who deal with this problem.

What about capital punishment? The Spirit World says that one murder does not justify another and that we must distinguish between punishment and revenge. We are indulging in the old idea of an eye for an eye and a tooth for a tooth. Punishment must be remedial and redemptive. Remember that there is no such thing as death and we are sending into the next world an undeveloped angry spirit filled with hatred. Such a spirit can create much harm in the next world (and in our world) because they can become earthbound and try to incite others still on the earth to sin and commit acts of cruelty. We are all familiar with the expressions "he was not himself", "I don't know what got into him" "he seemed possessed." There are no "evil spirits" — just the spirits of evil people burning with rage at what has happened to them. The spirit world thinks that we should do all we can to reform these people before they enter the next world. The workers in the next world have enough to cope with dealing with all the souls who are arriving every day and who are in a state of panic, disbelief, grief and rage. They are lost and bewildered and many have been brainwashed by their religion into certain beliefs about the next world.

What about accidental deaths and national disasters? Well spirit helpers are sent out to assist these souls who have been catapulted unexpectedly into the next world. (As I write these words the world is involved with helping the victims of the Tsumani.) Everyone is met and there is a very good organization in the next world which deals with the reception of newly arrived souls. Is the time of our passing known? Well those who are close to you know when you are coming and will be ready. Quite often people who are nearing death will say that they have seen a relative or relatives and this is because their spirit is getting ready to depart. I held my father's hand as he lay dying from a heart attack. He looked past me and said "I see you, I see you." It was only later that I realised that he was seeing members of his family who had come to escort him into the next world. Pope John Paul was heard to say something similar as he lay dying in the Vatican. "I have looked for you. Now you have come to me and I thank you." No doubt as he lay near to death he thought of his family and friends who had gone before him into the next world and how nice to know that they had come for him. A spirit doctor has said that when a person is dying his soul automatically knows that it is about to leave the body and a call goes out to loved ones in the next world who are then ready and waiting to receive them. In the case of an accident he says that the call goes out a split second before the soul leaves the body. The soul is aware of its passing in that split second and feels no pain.

Many people wonder if cremation or burial is best and of course the wishes of the deceased must be considered. In many ways cremation is better as it stops those left behind continually looking back over a plot of earth. My parents are buried (it was their wish) and I visit their grave with flowers but I know that they are not there! I heard a recently bereaved person saying how upset they were to witness heavy showers of rain coming down on the grave of a loved one and I longed to say to them "but they are not there!" I also read an article which told how some famous people keep by their beds the casket containing the ashes of a loved one. I think this is a completely morbid idea and they should realise that nothing can ever separate them from a loved one and if they want proof of this they should consult a good spiritualist medium where hopefully the loved one would make contact and give evidence of continued survival.

Spiritualism is not about death — it is about life eternal! We all existed as a spirit before we came into this world. We are a spirit inside a physical body and we don't just become a "spirit" when we die. Death may be the end of the life you are living in this world but it is the beginning of a new and glorious life in the next world. The Salvation Army calls it "promoted to glory." The grave has no power to end life and love is stronger than death. Living is a temporary state but love is forever. In some religions they teach that there is survival only for those who believe in certain doctrines and creeds but survival has nothing to do with religion. It is an automatic law and by the way, beloved pets will be waiting for you when you get there! Let us all live and enjoy our life on earth to the utmost and let's stop being afraid of death.

CHAPTER 6
WHAT I BELIEVE ABOUT THE NEXT WORLD

Everyone of us wants to know what the next world is like because one day everyone of us will be there! The only people who can tell us what it is like in the next world are those who are already living there and this is where Spiritualism comes into its own. The Church is of no help as we are simply told to "have faith" but I don't want to have faith I want TO KNOW! Who exactly gets into the next world? Is a special ticket or "Pass" needed that you show St Peter at the Pearly Gates? The various churches would have you believe that it is only if you accept certain teachings and follow certain rituals that you will gain entrance but no religion or church has been given the sole right to grant anyone entrance to heaven. They speak of a HEAVEN where the "Saved" will go and of a HELL where the "Unsaved" and others who do not accept their teachings will end up. All this is completely untrue. Many people think that they will only reach God by going through Jesus and that Jesus is some sort of a "bridge" to God. If this were so think of all the millions who are not Christians who would be excluded from the next world! It is not what you believe but what you have done with your life that counts. Spiritualists know with utter certainty that everyone goes into the next world — members of all religions and none. Faith and creeds have no say in the matter. The Spirit World is greater than every religion and every creed rolled into one. When you get there expect to meet people of other races, nations and religions. Expect to meet Atheists (who don't believe that God exists), Humanists, (who believe that when you are dead, you're dead!) Agnostics, (who don't know what to believe!) and also those who have never had a chance to consider the matter one way or another. The atheist will find proof of God in the next world. He will get a shock on his arrival but then so will our religious leaders! You were born into this world and you will also be born into the next world. It is automatic! Even if you don't want to survive you have no choice. You are an immortal being and you cannot die — you are indestructible! The Spirit World is open to the whole race of humanity but, more than that, it is open to every creature who has ever lived on this earth so don't be surprised to see Rover wagging his tail at you and Tiddles wrapping herself round your legs. I read this line in a spiritual book and I have never forgotten it — "What sort of Heaven would Heaven be, without my pets there to welcome me?" I have never had a pet but I have fed generations of garden birds in my lifetime and there is a certain little blackbird I look forward to meeting again.

There is however one qualification that you should be aware of when entering the next world and this has to do with "which part" of it you will be sent to. The next world is composed of people who come to it from the earth — the good, the bad, the clever, the uneducated and in fact just every type of person you could meet on the earth. There just has to be a sifting process because everybody would not be happy in the same place. The deciding factor has nothing to do with what sort of an education you have had, how much money you have earned, what sort of a job you have held down. In the eyes of spirit none of these things are of any real importance. The decision on where you will go depends entirely on the sort of person you are and the sort of life you have led. Have you led a life in which you have used the talents and opportunities given to you by God? Have you tried honestly to live a good life, following the teachings of Jesus Christ who was the most perfect of all human beings. Have you been loving and kind, caring and understanding, sympathetic and generous. The list is endless. Have you done the best you could with the deck of cards that life has dealt you and in the circumstances in which you found yourself? Jesus has told us a little about the next world. He said "In my Father's house there are many mansions." [John 14:2] Spiritualists interpret these "many mansions" to mean "many levels" and indeed this is what our Spirit Guides and masters from the next world teach us. The next world is not composed of simply a Heaven and a Hell. It is made up of different levels and the level that you will go to depends on your actions here on this earth. The next world is a graded one and of course we have not all reached the same grade in our spiritual development. When you return home to spirit you go to the level for which you are fitted because you have earned the right to be there and once there you will meet other souls at a similar stage to yourself. However you are not there "for keeps" and at some point you will feel the urge to move onward and upward although it could be a long time before this point is reached. Many people worry that when they reach the next world their loved ones will have progressed so far that they will never meet up with them. Our Spirit teachers tell us that while it is not possible for us to move up before we are ready, those higher up can certainly come down to our level and indeed many advanced souls do spend time on lower levels, teaching and helping those who live there. So never fear that you will not meet up with family and friends again.

36

Is there indeed a Heaven and a Hell as many of us have been taught to believe? The lowest level is where all those who have lived really evil lives will go and it is a very unpleasant place indeed. They will live among like-minded people — those murderers, rapists, child-abusers and all who have lived a bad life. Anyone sent to this level will find it a hell of their own creation caused by how they have lived their earthly lives. Remember however that life is all about progressing to perfection so, even these dregs of humanity will be given encouragement to see the evil of their ways, to make restitution and to advance up the ladder. Spirit workers in the next world will visit these lower levels to give help to these unadvanced souls. The Bible tells us that Jesus preached to these souls in hell before he rose from the dead. Dr Leslie Weatherhead, who is one of my favourite religious authors, has put it this way. "The whole purpose of state punishment is to make a wrong-doer into a useful member of society. If we believe in an endless hell this is just not possible. Punishment should lead to penitence and a new beginning. Jesus taught us that God is our Father and no father would go on punishing a child for the rest of his or her life".

What about those saintly people who have lived wonderful self-sacrificing lives? Well, they will go to one of the higher levels where they will enjoy the rewards of a life well-lived. God made the laws and a sinner cannot be put on the same spiritual level as a saint. The next world is not a static world. Everyone is on the move striving ever upwards (like climbing a spiral staircase) to reach higher and higher planes. Will we see God in the next world? I remember the words of Jesus about only the pure in heart seeing God [Matt. 5:8] and I think it will take us all a long, long time before we reach that level if indeed we ever do. We are told that we will continue to progress for countless ages (everyone is somewhere on the ladder) and Silver Birch says he knows nothing of "endings". However I do expect to meet Jesus who said "where I am, there ye may be also."[John, 14:3] Many questions are put to our spirit guides about Jesus. They are asked if they have met him, where is he now and what is he doing. The answers are that he is still working in the next world and that he is the head of our movement to bring the true knowledge of God to humanity but that he weeps bitter, bitter tears at what has happened to the beautiful message of God's love that he brought down to earth.

The majority of people in this world are neither saints nor sinners so where do we "ordinary" souls go to in the next world? Well our spirit guides tell us that we go to what is known as the "Astral" plane and that this plane is very similar to earth and contains duplicates of everything on earth. You will see buildings, houses, gardens, lakes, countryside, birds and other animals (and I would not want a heaven that did not include the song of birds.) In fact so like the earth is this world that some people do not realize that they are dead! Life on this level is just as solid and real as life on earth but it is far more beautiful. There is a well-known spirit book called "Life in the World Unseen" by Anthony Borgia. He says that many souls arriving from the earth are shocked to find a solid substantial world with real live people in it. They think it is far too much like earth with its houses and buildings and not at all like a world of eternal rest which so many expect it to be. There will be no singing hymns around the throne of God! New arrivals will certainly rest until they are restored to full strength but then they will want to do something useful, perhaps carry on with work like they had on earth and also take advantage of the opportunities now open to them. There is really so much to look forward to in the Spirit World. You will not live a lazy idle life or be bored.

Someone said to Silver Birch that he had always wanted to play the piano and could he learn in the next world. He was assured that this was possible as there were teachers available for every subject. We are told of beautiful gardens, flowers, countryside, pets, "Halls of Learning" where we can study and learn to our hearts content under the best teachers the world has ever known. There are Concert Halls where musicians can entertain us and wonderful libraries housing the books of all the ages. At one spiritualist meeting I attended one of the congregation was receiving a message from her father in the next world. The medium said to her "your father was fond of books." "Oh yes" was the reply "he was a great reader." "Well" said the medium "he says just wait till you see the libraries we have over here!" We are told of museum like buildings in which are kept a record of every country, every civilization and every aspect of the world since it began. Well at last we will be able to find out the truth about things that have puzzled us in our history. What really did happen to Atlantis? What about churches? Yes, there will still be churches because when people cross over they are still sectarian in their beliefs but eventually they realize that there is only one God for all. How do we communicate in the next world? There is no speech because communication is through telepathy or as a little spirit girl explained it in a typically childish way "we speak with our think!" This of course makes it easy to speak to those from other countries whose native language is different from your own. What about food? Well food is available but after a while you no longer want it so I don't suppose there will be any slimming clubs in the next world!

What will people look like in the next world? Well you are already a spiritual being. You don't get a spirit body when you die because you have it now! The spirit body is a replica of your physical body and it emerges intact at death without the physical defects of its earthly counterpart. There will be no need for spectacles or false teeth, no missing limbs and no deformities physical or mental. My father was a little hard of hearing before he died. In a message I got from him he said he could now hear even the grass growing! Sometimes when a medium is receiving a message from someone in the next world he/she will mention a physical deformity in order to identify the person (eg this lady lived all her life with one leg shorter than the other). These things are mentioned purely for identification purposes and everyone has a perfect body in the next world. You will still have all your senses. You will wear clothes and I have read that most people wear a long flowing toga of different colours. Indeed a Leslie Flint communicator spoke of wearing a "Roman toga" and I imagine that fashion is not an important issue in the next world! You will still have your jewellery and other personal possessions because there are duplicates of everything in the next world. After death you are still you. You don't change and this is why we recognise our loved ones when they communicate with us. Whatever you had in the way of brains and character you take with you but you do not suddenly become all wise and know all the answers. You are just the same as you were on earth with the same thoughts, ideas and memories. To put it bluntly — if someone was a selfish, unkind and nasty person while on earth then they will not become an instant angel in the next world! They will have to learn to change their ways because spirit life is all about progressing to perfection and every level you progress to is more beautiful than the last.

There is no growing old in the next world for age disappears. Children will grow to maturity but the aged will revert to the prime of life. Women will become younger and regain their looks and men will regain their strength. What about marriage? If there is true love then partners will progress together but if the love is only superficial then eventually they will go their separate ways. Love is the greatest binding force in the universe and if two people really love one another nothing will ever come between them. The Prayer Book is wrong with its "till death us do part." If two people love one another there can be no parting.

So what do we all do in our new life? White Eagle, another of our spirit teachers, says that in the next world you work when you want to and play when you want to. However after a while everybody finds out that they want to work, to learn and to have a chance to do all the things that they were never able to do while on the earth. I have lately become aware of the paintings of Thomas Kincade. This gentleman is a committed Christian and he is known as the "painter of light." To me some of his paintings of nature truly give a glimpse of heaven. He has said "imagine a life where there is plenty of time, plenty of energy, plenty of opportunity for everything you feel is important — plus a little left over for some things you simply enjoy." What a wonderful picture that is of Heaven! I have always felt that if I lived a dozen lives I still could not do and experience all the things I want. I could not read all the books I want to read, visit all the countries in the world I would like to see, learn all the subjects I am interested in and enjoy all the hobbies I would like to. In short I cannot experience everything in one short earth life which those in the Spirit World tell us is just a few seconds on the time scale of eternity. I look forward to going to the next world where I will have all the time in the world to do what I want to do. In the next world you will not be pushed into a job of work which you find boring. You are chosen for a task which will be just right for you. It will be a wonderful world because everyone will be doing work that they love and there will be no square pegs in round holes. All the knowledge, skills and talents that you acquired on earth can still be used to help those still on the earthplane. In my career as a librarian I was always aware of someone putting ideas into my head on how best to tackle certain tasks. I have asked the next world for help in many ways from dress-making to DIY and always the help has come either by encountering someone on the earth who could help me or by direct voice communication and by visual pictures sent from the next world. Everyone of us has gone through training of some sort for our job in life and from the next world we can pass on our knowledge to those still on the earth who are struggling to cope. Doctors and nurses will try to help their earthly counterparts, academics involved in research will try to work with others engaged on similar tasks. I hope that what I have just said will comfort those who have lost a young relative who died before they had a chance to fulfil their potential in life. It is always sad to read in the newspapers of a clever person who has died young but all our learning, talents and abilities will not go to waste in the next world. Remember that every new discovery or invention on the earth has first to come from the next world. Ideas do not spring into men's minds accidentally for all come from God through His servants and they are all good ideas. It is man who distorts them and makes them evil. Books, films, television, videos, the internet are all wonderful but if used incorrectly can be a cause of evil. Children who arrive in the next world have to be cared for. Children who die young do not automatically go the highest sphere because, although they have not been contaminated by the earth and are really quite pure, they have lost out on all the experience and knowledge that a life on earth can give. They go to a very special place where they will be trained and educated by those specially chosen for this work. Then there are also pet animals and poor unwanted ill-treated pets need special care. I remember hearing someone get a message once from a friend who had recently died. The medium told her that she could see her friend in the next world and that she was surrounded by cats! "Oh" said the recipient "she always loved cats and she worked for a cat charity before she died." So there was one new arrival in the next world who had stepped straight into the perfect job! Every day people are arriving in this new world. They are bewildered confused and dazed and they need a great deal of help to settle down. Those who pass on beds of sickness will awaken in a spirit hospital — not that they are still sick — but it is less of a shock to them when they open their eyes and they need some attention before they can start their new life. God is kind and all awake to scenes of familiarity where loved ones are waiting to welcome them. Of course some people have the fixed idea in their head that they will sleep till Judgment Day and not awaken until Gabriel blows his horn! Ramadan (another spirit teacher) tells the amusing story of how they awaken such people by fetching a spirit musician and having him blow a horn!

Many people think that Spiritualism is concerned too much with death and dying. The job of Spiritualism is to tell you how important it is to live a good, full and useful life in the here and now because it is an important factor in how you will spend eternity. According to the way you live your life on the earth and the way you deal with your problems you can at least get a foothold on the spiritual ladder and perhaps even climb a rung or two on it. Jesus was the ideal example of how we should live our lives but sadly we are told to worship him as a God rather than model our lives on his. You are born into this world to learn lessons and gain experience in this school of life. It is not until most people reach the next world that they really find out what life is all about. Millions of people go through their life on this earth without the faintest idea of what lies ahead. All religions are basically the same and we are all making for the same end but we just give that end a different name. At death our eyes are opened and we start to realize that we belong not to one nation, not to one race, not to one faith but to the one family of God.

In the next world you will be absolutely safe for nothing can hurt you. You will never again feel lonely or unloved, unwanted or unneeded for you will be surrounded by those who love and understand you. You will never feel that "you don't belong" for you will be in a place which is just right for you and where you will fit in. You will choose how to occupy your time and life will open up for you in a very wonderful way. Moreover you will have all eternity to enjoy it. There is really nothing to fear about going into the next world — because you see you are just "going home!"

CHAPTER 7
WHAT I BELIEVE ABOUT SIN AND JUDGMENT

Sin, now there's a good old-fashioned word! Just what is sin? My dictionary defines sin as the "wilful transgression of divine law." Man also has created laws (parking on double-yellow lines, not paying for a TV licence) and these laws if broken will have have earthly consequences but it is with the breaking of God's laws that that this chapter is concerned.

The Bible has a lot to say about sin including what is known as the seven deadly sins. These are Pride (holding too high an opinion of yourself), Covetousness (a longing to possess what belongs to another), Lust (sexual desire), Gluttony (being greedy and overeating), Anger (rage and violent displeasure), Envy (feeling pain at another's success) and Sloth (laziness.) Well we are all certainly guilty of some of these to a greater or lesser extent. While there is nothing wrong with feeling proud of your achievements you should remember that perhaps others did not have the same opportunities as you did. Covetousness would account for much of modern day crime like theft, burglary, shoplifting etc where the thought is "I see, I want and I take." Lust is the cause of rape, sexual abuse and contributes to the breakdown of marriages. Gluttony is certainly responsible for the current obesity crisis in affluent nations. Anger can lead to murder and grievous bodily harm. Envy, with its companion jealousy, can lead to destruction of others possessions while sloth (laziness) is very evident in the world today where so many think that life owes them a living and are reluctant to study and work hard.

However there are also sins of omission as well as sins of commission. You are just as much a sinner if you omit or refuse to do something to help. Remember the parable of the rich man in his house and the beggar Lazarus at his gate? The rich man could have done something to help poor Lazarus but he did nothing. Therefore he sinned. Again in the parable of the Good Samaritan [Luke 10:30-37] those who passed by the robbed and injured man without offering help were all sinners in the eyes of God. Over and over again in life we are given chances to help someone in some way and if we refuse these chances — turn a blind eye — then we will one day have to answer for that which we failed to do.

The Bible says that "all have sinned and come short of the glory of God." [Rom. 3:23] Well there is no argument about that but we are put on this earth to learn the lessons of life, one of which is to overcome sin and temptation and if you were a perfect person you would not be on the earth in the first place! Jesus was the only completely sinless person to have ever been born into this world. He was a highly evolved soul who had reached the peak of perfection and he did say "what I have done, ye can do also" [John 14:12]. One of the seven Principles of Spiritualism is "Personal Responsibility." God has given you free-will and you cannot have free-will without taking the responsibility for your actions. Do not excuse your failures by saying that "it was not God's will." Spiritualists believe that each and everyone of us is entirely responsible for the life we lead, the decisions we make, the words we speak and the actions we take. We have all been given a conscience that tells us the difference between right and wrong and we all have to choose to do good or evil. So — why does God allow evil? I don't think He allows it but He has given us all free-will and He cannot interfere to stop it otherwise we would be like "puppets on a string." The German philosopher F. Neisher has said that the idea of evil is nothing more than an excuse for mankind to avoid taking responsibility for the bad things that happen, or, as Archbishop Rowan Williams has put it— "it lets us off the hook." Archbishop Desmond Tutu says that God has a profound reverence for our freedom as individuals and, while He must sometimes weep at the state of the world, He must leave us free to make our own choices. If you want to progress up the spiritual ladder to perfection then you must accept sole responsibility for what you do with your life. The Ten Commandments spell out the basic rules of human behaviour and the "Sermon on the Mount" gave us more rules for how we should conduct ourselves.

Spiritualists do not believe that Jesus died "to wash away our sins" as the old hymn says. They believe that everyone must answer for their own sins and it is this principle above all others which differentiates Spiritualism from the Christian faith. Spiritualists look upon the life of Jesus Christ as a superb example of how to live but they do not believe that his death made atonement for the sins of humanity. We believe that life is eternal so the soul has all eternity to remove its imperfections. How can anyone believe in a loving God who required a horrible human sacrifice before He could become reconciled to His people? What would we think of a human father who, before he would forgive his little son or daughter for some

44

misdeed, told them that they must put a beloved pet to a tortuous death? Such behaviour would forever kill any affection between the father and his children. Yet this is what the churches would have us believe? As a child I found it hard to believe that Jesus had "died for my sins." The older I became and the more I pondered religion the harder I found it to swallow this belief. I believe that God loves each and everyone of us, even the most depraved of characters. I believe He forgives us our sins and that His love will never end but — while sin is forgiven — the consequences of sin must be faced up to and restitution made. God hates the sin but loves the sinner. The sinner must be brought to a realization of exactly what his action has resulted in and his soul must take steps — from the next world if necessary — to make amends. Progress towards God is not possible without repentance and restitution.

Another of the Seven Principles of Spiritualism is "Compensation and Retribution hereafter for every good and evil deed done on earth." What about judgment? Well the Bible itself does say "Whatsoever a man soweth that shall he also reap."[Gal. 6:7] Christianity would have us believe that saints and sinners will be treated equally but this is not divine justice. Should Hitler occupy the same place in the next world as Mother Theresa? God made the laws of this world and no one is allowed to cheat and "get away with it." It may seem from our earthly standpoint that many in this world do "get away with it." We feel indignant at the short sentences meted out to criminals but they will receive their just desserts in the next world for we must all answer one day to a higher justice. In fact criminals will pay twice for their sins because there is God's judgment to face even after they have paid for the sin on earth. Silver Birch says that our world is full of injustices but that the spiritual ledger is always balanced. Perhaps if everyone understood this then we might have fewer criminals and a better world. Spiritualists believe in "cause and effect" which is like the biblical "reaping and sowing." Once we arrive in the next world we will become aware of the effect that our life has had on others. Edgar Cayce, the great psychic, has phrased it very well when he spoke of "standing at the judgment bar of your own conscience." You yourself will assess your life with the help of an understanding teacher. We will be shown pictures of our past life and we can see what we were really like. We will feel the thoughts and feelings that our actions and words have caused in the life of others. We will all see what has resulted from these actions and words for this is the law and there are no exceptions to the rule. The gospel of Matthew Chpt 12 verse 36 tells us that Jesus said "Every idle word that men shall speak they shall give account thereof in the day of judgment." Every thought, word and deed which we have performed in our earthly life is stored on a video in our sub-conscious mind and after death we will see this video and watch a review of our life. People who have had a very close encounter with death often speak of seeing their whole life flash before their eyes. I think that seeing this video could be a very painful experience and knowing that I will have to face this review of my life helps to keep me constantly aware of how I behave in this world. If everyone realised that there is a life after this one and that they would have to face this judgment of self then their behaviour patterns would change. This is surely a better incentive to live a good life than the teachings of the Christian church which more or less tells you to live as you want because at the end of the day "Jesus died for your sins." Spiritualism teaches a clear system of reward and punishment but not of a paradise and a brutal hell. The news is not all bad however because you will also see how the kind actions and words you gave out help to balance the account and there will be counsellors there to help us through this experience and give us love and understanding. When this judgment is complete the spirit will go to the home it has made for itself and from there it will progress to yet higher heavens. There is no flaming torturing Hell into which sinners are cast. This is an invention of the church. Through the ages it has frightened its followers by speaking of Hell, damnation and a day of judgment. Anyone committing a crime in today's world and coming before a judge and jury is usually provided with background reports which try to explain why the offender committed the crime. Well God knows you better than any background report! Even the hairs on your head are numbered! [Matt 10:30] He knows the influences that came to bear on your life, He knows all about your disappointments and what made you lose your joy in life, He understands what made you the person you are and His is the best judgment you will ever face. In the world we are all going to some day, all is known, understood and forgiven but sin must be repented and wrongs righted before advancement in the heavenly spheres is possible.

Remember that in the next world you will not be judged by how much money you made in your life, how many possessions you had, how many academic degrees you acquired or what your status was. However where the privileges have been greatest there the judgment will be sternest or, to put it another way, to whom much is given, much will be required. "For unto whomsoever much is given, of him shall be much required." [Luke 12:48]. You will be judged on what you did with your life. Did you make good use of your talents or did you miss your opportunities? The Parable of the Talents in the Bible tells how the one who hid his in the ground was taken to task and that talent was given to another. [Matt. 25:28] So — in your own life what have you done to make the world a better place? Is the world a better place because you have lived in it? Have you sent a Christmas card to a lonely person. Have you been kind to a new neighbour or new work mate? Have you visited a housebound person or someone in a hospital or nursing home? Have you fed the birds in the garden particularly during a cold winter spell? Jesus said "inasmuch as you have done it unto one of the least of these my brethren ye have done it unto me." [Matt 25:40] A visiting medium at my church quoted these words in his address.

When the Great Scorer comes
To write across your name.
It won't be about winning
But how you played the game.

That I think sums it up very nicely!

We are all brought up to believe that the "goodies" go to heaven and the "baddies" go to hell. However few of us are so good that we deserve heaven and I hope that few of us are numbered amongst the really evil people of this world who deserve to go to hell. So — who does decide where we end up in the next world? Well it is not God sitting on some throne dispensing rewards and punishments to each soul. There is an automatic law to deal with the affects of your actions while you are on the earth plane. It is an absolutely fair system of judgment and one with which every right-minded person should agree. Christianity would have us believe that a death-bed repentance allows the most evil sinner to enter paradise alongside those who have lived good lives and served their fellow men. This would be a complete mockery of the laws of God and God's Law is perfect. Each person will receive exactly that to which he is entitled. Our spirit guides tell us that the next world consists of a number of interlocking spheres (or levels of existences) and we go to the particular level that our life on earth has fitted us for. Thoroughly bad people go to the lowest astral level when they die. Such people are among those like themselves and see their own vices reflected all around them. They would not be happy in a sphere of more purity and would yearn for old haunts and habits.

So — what about those in this lowest level? Is there no hope for them? Of course there is! We are told that Jesus descended into Hell to preach to these souls and other highly evolved teachers visit this sphere to give instruction and continually strive to bring these sinners to a sense of what they have done wrong. In this world we send wrongdoers to prison and while there we try to reform them to lead better lives on their release and this is what happens to the souls in the lowest sphere although it may take thousands of years before they begin to realize the wrong they have done and become ready to move on. How can someone be reformed if he or she is cast into an everlasting Hell. Lord Dowding has said that an idea of what is going to happen at death should have an improving effect on the way we live our present lives. While spiritualists do not believe in a fiery hell to which evil souls are sent for eternity they do believe that each soul must come to a realization of their wrongdoing and set about making amends.

Spiritualist teaching about sin and judgment is more likely to deter people from sinning than the church's teaching. We hold out hope of renewed chances. Spiritualists know beyond any shadow of doubt that there is a world after this world. We know that when we go there we will assess our lives. We will look at the things we learned and those we did not learn. Did we make good use of the life God had given to us or did we waste our time. We know that there will be glorious reunions and an opportunity to say "Sorry." We know that we will have all eternity to fulfil our potential for the 7th Principle of Spiritualism is "Eternal Progress open to every soul."

CHAPTER 8
WHAT I BELIEVE ABOUT THE CHRISTIAN RELIGION

During my life I have attended churches of many different Christian denominations. I was baptised and brought up as a member of the Episcopal Church of Scotland. However I also went with my school chums to the local Church of Scotland Sunday School and of course like all Scottish schoolchildren of the 'forties I received a great deal of religious instruction while in primary school. I was made to memorize Psalms and Paraphrases which I can still recite to this day. A close schoolfriend was a Baptist so I was influenced by her religious convictions and indeed I have always felt the strongest admiration for Dr Billy Graham. During my career I worked with and made friends of Roman Catholics, Methodists, Unitarians as well as non-believers like Humanists, Atheists and Agnostics. For a while I attended meetings of the Salvation Army — an organization which I greatly admire and I have been involved in Bible Study Groups and I certainly learned a lot about the good book from them. However, while I admired the sincerity of these churches, their teachings of a blind belief in certain creeds and the following of certain rituals in no way gave to my life the meaning or purpose for which I sought. My mother had attended Spiritualist meetings as a young woman (with her mother) so I knew about them and in fact I attended my first Spiritualist meeting when I was 18.

Many people accept their church's teachings and never think things out for themselves. This is something I have never been able to do even as a child. I was taught that I was a sinner (which I quite accept) although I do not accept that I was born into sin. What a start that is for anyone's life? I was told that Jesus had died on the cross to absolve me from my sins. I must have been quite a strong-minded little girl because this did not make sense to me. If I had done wrong then surely I was the one to be punished not this glorious sinless man who preached about a God and a Father who loved us all. At school in our history lessons we had heard of the "whipping boy". If the son of the house committed a wrong then instead of him getting the whipping another boy was chosen to receive it instead. "How unfair" we all thought and yet here was the church teaching that Jesus was God's whipping boy. How could this horrible God be the same one that Jesus had told us about? Jesus told of a God of tenderness, pity and love. Certainly not one who required a cruel human sacrifice like this. In the parable of the Prodigal Son [Luke 15:11-32] he compared God to a loving father, a father who still loved and welcomed his son home after all the sins he had committed. He also compared Him to the good shepherd who went in search of the lost sheep [Luke 15:3-7]. The churches preached that unless I accepted that Jesus had died for my sins then I would not enter the Kingdom of Heaven. But what about the little baby who dies after taking only a few breaths of life? What about the heathen who had never heard the gospel? What about the mentally ill who were incapable of understanding anything? Also, was it fair that those who had lived a wicked life could say with their dying breath that they believed that Jesus had died for their sins and enjoy paradise just the same as someone who had led a saintly life on this earth? No, no, none of this made sense to me. I believed in justice for all, albeit tempered with mercy.

The churches would have us accept things with a blind belief or faith. I believe that God gave us all powers of reasoning and that we should not accept anything we are told unless it makes sense to us. Spiritualist guides in the next world tell us that we must always question, never accept blindly and apply reasoning to everything. Now this is just the opposite of what the churches teach! They insist that we must believe in their teachings or be damned for eternity. The job of churches should be to educate people about God and not to indoctrinate them and far too many people today have been brainwashed by being told what they must believe. Man must seek the truth for himself. Richard Holloway, former Bishop of Edinburgh, has said that religion is used as a substitute for God and not as a way to God and that if we want to know God then we must get rid of God substitutes. In the past the church has decided what is right, what is wrong, what is sin. This does not allow each person to think things out for themselves. Look at history to see all the people who were murdered by church authorities because they would not believe what they were told and Jesus is the prime example because he dared to differ with the religious authorities of his day. Many people today say that they have lost their faith in God but it was never their faith in the first place — it was somebody else's! There is a saying "God has no grandchildren" and this means that we should not accept our belief in God because it is our parents' belief. We must arrive at our own conclusions. If your faith is your own and it has been tried and tested then it will never leave you in your hour of need.

Your religious background is a result of where you were born, your national culture and what you were taught by your parents. For some people the faith that they have been brought up in is satisfying for them and they hate being disturbed in their convictions and prefer to stick to the traditional path. However many people today can no longer accept the church's teachings and they question its authority. All of us have changed our views about God since we grew up. Today's church is condemning you to a form of religion which may have suited your ancestors but which is quite unsuited to the man or woman in this modern world. Sometimes the church tries to change its teachings to suit the spirit of the age. They take a stand on various issues to try to appear progressive and open-minded. They become liberal in moral matters and ignore the words of their own Bible which states quite clearly for example that fornication and adultery are sins. Jesus spoke the truth whether it was popular or not. It is wrong to change Bible teachings to suit popular thinking.

Churches are losing their congregations because they do not make God relevant to men and women of today. Until the churches put this idea across they will continue to lose members. Dr William Barclay said that the test of anything is "Does it work?" Well obviously the churches do not! Religion must be seen to work. Churches everywhere are closing down as congregations dwindle. The church has forgotten the original message of Jesus and in so doing has lost the support of many. In the city where I live unused churches have been turned into nightclubs, restaurants, sports clubs, new flats etc. People these days are more educated than previous generations and will not blindly accept the church's teachings. Also — do those who are regular attenders really believe? I remember a work colleague who was a fervent attender of her church — choir, youth club, etc — telling me of the death of a close friend. "It's the end, the end" she kept saying. I said to her "but don't you believe she has gone to Heaven?" Her face flushed with embarrassment. " Er oh yes, oh yes, of course" she said but she had evidently never really thought it out. I had always wanted to visit the Holy Land and see the places mentioned in the Bible. I had my holiday booked and I said to a friend who was a pillar of her church — women's guild, choir etc — "wouldn't you like to go also?" "No, I'm not interested" was her reply. Not interested — in the country of your God! I have long thought that many people attend church just for the social organizations they run. To me this is very wrong. You should go to church to worship God. I think the churches should stick to their job of teaching people about God and His laws for living and leave socializing groups to outside bodies.

I do think that we need churches in the world. We need an organized body to teach humanity God's rules for living. There are many different religions in the world but there is only one God and today's world needs God! Men and women need to know that they matter, that someone cares that they are tired, despondent, have suffered a disappointment, feel sneered at, belittled and discouraged. They need to be told that even if the whole world turns against them they are still precious in the eyes of God. People today no longer have faith in the ability of the church to answer their problems. Religion is separated from everyday life and few carry their church's teachings into their day-to-day life. Silver Birch says "Do not speak to me of Christians whose lives mock the one they profess to serve." There are "Sunday Christians" who pay lip service to a God whose teachings they have no intention of following during the rest of the week. This notion was beautifully expressed in an episode of "To the Manor Born", Audrey Forbes-Hamilton takes Richard de Vere to task for not going to church. "Why were you not at church?" "I am not religious." "What has that got to do with it?"

The God we worship today is a modern God of the 21st Century who is entirely familiar with our technological age. He is not a God who spoke through Jesus over 2000 years ago and has remained silent ever since. Revelation is ongoing. The churches insist on a blind belief in doctrines worked out hundreds of years ago. The church still uses a form of worship it has used for centuries and some of its language is positively archaic — people do not speak like that today. I welcome the new versions of the Bible which we now have but it has taken a long time for these to be available. When I was a child the Bible in regular use had been brought out in 1611 and used the language that was used by the people of that time. This stopped many people from reading the Bible. The church also concentrates too much on pomp, ceremony and rituals but does this bring us any nearer to the reality of God? Churches gather their own members into a community which separates them from other believers. They raise more barriers than they break down. Some church members repel us because of their self-righteousness and unchristian behaviour. "Calls himself a Christian!" I think we all expect a certain standard of behaviour from followers of religious beliefs. In other words we judge their heavenly God by their worldly behaviour. Everyone needs a standard with which to compare his or her self. Jesus can be that standard. Would Jesus have had someone burned at the stake because that person did not accept his teachings about God? Would Jesus tell a grieving mother that her baby would go to Hell because that baby had not been baptised? Silver Birch says "The Great Spirit (as he calls God) is not troubled if a man has sprinkled water or not." What does matter, he says, is that the new life is lived according to the highest ideals and you cannot cheat God's law because a few drops of water are sprinkled on a baby's head. Now I think that to have a baby christened is a very nice little ceremony in which family and friends can welcome that new little soul into our world but in no way does it affect that child's ultimate entrance into the next world. The Church teaches that each baby is born with the blemish of Adam's original sin and so is tarnished in the eyes of God. They say that after death even a new born child has to make atonement to God. What utter rubbish! What could be more innocent than a newborn infant!

We read today in our newspapers of Nuns abusing children in their care. These nuns are followers of a man who said "Suffer the little children to come unto me for of such is the Kingdom of heaven." [Matt 19:14] We also read of priests sexually abusing young boys from their parish. How can anyone respect a religious organization where such things are going on? If the church wants to influence us all to live good lives and make a better world then it had better clean up it's own act first. I find it hard to understand how Christian churches can preach of a saviour god dying on the cross for the forgiveness of sins. Surely in their theological studies to become priests they have had to study the history of other religions and they must realize that "Saviour Gods" abound in the old pagan religions. (Type the words "Saviour Gods" into Google and see what the Internet brings up!) All these gods it was claimed were born of virgins, performed miraculous deeds and ended up dying as martyrs. When I read things like this I really wonder about the true life of Jesus. His life seems to be confused with the myths and legends of previous gods. Our savage ancestors could only think in terms of savage gods who needed to be constantly pacified with sacrifices, burnt offerings and torture of those who refused to believe. They also believed that if they ate the body and drank the blood of the sacrificed one they would be endowed with good qualities. Today civilized people are still taking part in ceremonies where they "eat" their God "Body of Christ" and "Drink" his blood and they just do not seem to realize that they are taking part in what was once a pagan ceremony. Priests today claim that a wafer of bread and a drop of wine magically become the body and blood of Jesus. Some churches even refer to this ceremony as being "washed in the blood of the lamb." Now in this century the thought of drinking anyone's blood is disgusting and yet the churches would have us believe that this is what God wants us to do! If anyone reading this book thinks that they will not get into the next world because they do not take part in this ceremony then let me reassure them. My father never took it in his life and he is very much in the next world and has communicated with me on numerous occasions. I myself was confirmed at the age of 14 into the Episcopal Church of Scotland and I took communion two or three times and then decided I wanted nothing more to do with it. I know that God loves me very, very much and I have no fear that St Peter will bar me from entering through the pearly gates when my time comes. The taking of Holy Communion, the Lord's Supper or whatever you like to call it is in no way necessary for entrance into the next world. Remember that the Salvation Army, that most Christian of all organizations, does not have this "bread" and "blood" ceremony and neither do the Quakers or certain other Christian sects.

Religion has nothing to do with ritual and ceremony, with beautiful singing and chanting, with jewels and gorgeous raiment and vestments. It has nothing to do with stained glass windows, with beautifying the interior of a church, with statues and religious pictures. Religion should be a standard of conduct and not obedience to rituals and ceremonies. Religion is service — serving God by serving His children and this was the message of Jesus. Love one another he said over and over again but the church that was founded by his followers has divided mankind caused wars and bloodshed, torture and the dreaded inquisition. The Christian Church has committed terrible atrocities in the name of its founder. As the teachings of Jesus spread they became mixed up with other religious cults like Mithraism and took over many of their rites and festivals. The Church realised that they would be come unpopular if they dumped all the pagan festivals so they adopted and adapted them into the church. An Egyptian God was AMEN. He was identified with the Sun God and became RA-AMEN. After prayers people always said Amen and this word has come down to us in the Christian religion. The vestments worn by our priests are part of the Pharaoh's robes. These Egyptian gods always had a disc behind their heads to represent the sun. This has come down to us in the halo behind Jesus's head. Incense is another ritual which has come down to us from Egypt. The fumes were meant to convey to the Gods the spirits released

54

from the food offerings. Too much time is spent observing religious ceremonies. The church's doctrine that it alone knows the truth and can offer salvation by means of sacraments or else man is condemned to eternal hell is a terrible hold over mankind. It takes away all sense of personal responsibility and gives the impression that you can do what you want in life so long as you take the sacraments. No outward ceremony can wash away your past sins. God will always forgive you but only you can redeem yourself by making restitution. If you don't try to do this in this world then you will have to do it in the next for nobody "gets away with it." The task of religious leaders should be to convince their flock that if they commit wicked acts then they are going to be faced with retribution in the world to come. That they will have to atone for their crimes and seek forgiveness from those they have hurt in any way. The teaching of an eternal damnation in Hell will hardly draw people to God. They have to be told that God is love and that He will go on loving them despite their sins but that they must put right the wrongs they have done. The church is very wrong to preach that Jesus died for our sins. Spiritualism teaches that everyone must take responsibility for their own actions. There is an even greater wrong that the churches are teaching their followers and that is that Jesus is a God to be worshipped! Jesus is not a god, he was a messenger sent from God. Many times in the New Testament Jesus said that he was "sent" by God. As for example in [John 17:3] "...that they might know Thee the only true God, and Jesus Christ, whom Thou has sent." Think of the Ten Commandments. "Thou shalt have no other gods before me." What could be clearer than that! When Jesus was tempted by the devil he is reputed to have said "Thou shalt worship the Lord thy God and Him only shalt thou serve."[Matt 4:10]. When Jesus was addressed as "Good Master" by the rich young man he replied to him "Why do you call me good? No one is good but God." [Matt 19:16-17]. When he taught us how to pray he used the words "Our Father" so he was claiming to be one of us and he spoke of going to "My God and your God." Are these the words of someone who considered himself to be an equal of God? It saddens me when I watch "Songs of Praise" — that popular Sunday evening programme to notice how most of the hymns are about Jesus and only one or two about God. The spirit world has the greatest respect for Jesus whom they call the Nazarene but they say it is wrong to worship him for worship should only be given to the Great Spirit (God) and not to His messengers. One day the churches will have to answer for preaching that taking part in any ceremony, creed etc gives you advantage over others, that you do not have to make a personal effort to gain salvation and that Jesus is a god to be worshipped.

Everyone of us is making a journey through life and we all come from different religious backgrounds. Don't make your faith an excuse for not finding out the truth. Do not blindly accept what you have been taught but think it out for yourself. Some people think that what was good enough for their parents is good enough for them. They are not growing in their faith and their religious development is that of a child. Well — you would not go to a doctor who clung to old fashioned methods of treatment now would you? All religions regard their own sacred writings as the truth and they think that other religions are just myths. Richard Holloway has said that each tries to persuade that theirs is the only true religion and the way to God. However the golden grain of truth runs through all religions and Spiritualists will accept ideals from all religions and sacred writings. Orthodox religions rely solely on faith about what awaits us all in the next world but Spiritualism provides evidence and proof of survival by communicating with those who are already there. We know there is an afterlife because we have evidence of it. Tony Ortzen the editor of the Spiritualist Magazine "Two Worlds" says that one of Spiritualism's greatest strengths is that is is based on facts unlike other religions. He also says that the churches, by cutting themselves off from communication with the next world are denying themselves and their congregations the wisdom so readily available from there.

All the faiths in the whole world lead back to just one God. The Rev. James A. Simpson in his book "Holy Wit" tells of a child describing the difference between Jews, Protestants and Catholics who said "they are all just different ways of voting for God." I believe that religion is a continuing revelation about God but it is only given to us in proportion as we are prepared to receive it. There is much to understand about the meaning of life but we are not yet ready to learn it. Revelation from God is ongoing. We must all try to live a good life according to the teachings of Jesus and forget the superstitious nonsense that the churches have put on top of those teachings. Not to believe in religion does not mean not to believe in God. We must look to God and not to men for approval and our actions must be determined by our knowledge of God's laws and not man's. Spiritualism teaches that you can go to God direct and you do not need anyone else to intercede for you. He is your God just as much as your minister's or priest's and you don't need to go to a church to talk to Him!

The religion of the future should be built on known facts and not consist of a mix of myths and legends handed down to us over the centuries. It should be able to include the best of all religions and this is what Spiritualism is, for it is a universal religion. Being religious does not mean abandoning the world, giving up all the ease and comfort of life, becoming a hermit, reading nothing but the Bible. It means living a good, clean life by following God's rules for living which are eternal and unchanging. It means serving God by serving mankind and the other living creatures who share our life on this planet. It means looking after God's world, living your own life to the full, (100%) and extracting as much as you can from your time on this earth plane so that when the time comes for you to move onto the next phase of your existence you will truly hear the words "Well done, thou good and faithful servant, enter into the joy of the Lord."[Matt 25:21]

CHAPTER 9
WHAT I BELIEVE ABOUT SUFFERING.

There is an old saying that has come down to us through the ages and that is that "Suffering is good for the soul." This is exactly the teaching of the next world. We are placed on this earth so that our souls will grow. This is of small comfort to those who are suffering be it physical pain or mental anguish and it should be remembered also that it is not only bad people who suffer but good people also. Believers in God do not live idyllic lives but suffer as much as everyone else. Remember the verse in the Bible — "Though He slay me yet will I trust in Him" [Job 13:15] and just think about what poor Job had to go through! Nobody goes through an earthly life free from pain and suffering and the suffering is not always visible to the onlooker. Nobody wears their heart on their sleeve. Catherine Cookson, the famous novelist once spoke of the "courage behind the mask" and I thought what a very true saying that was because we all wear a mask in our daily life. How do any of us know what another person is feeling. One of the greatest failings of human beings is the inability to put themselves in another person's position. The outgoing confident person cannot understand the painfully shy one. The person who is the life and soul of the party cannot understand the awkward mixer who prefers to stay away. The overconscientious worker cannot switch off after leaving work as a more relaxed colleague can. Clever people are often impatient with those who are slow to learn and a physically fit person cannot understand the one who tires easily. Truly sympathetic people are those who have gone through such experiences themselves.

Suffering can be either physical or mental and, while physical pain is terrible to bear, at least these days medical science can prescribe drugs to alleviate pain. Mental and emotional suffering however is something that can be with you for ever. As usual Shakespeare had the right words for it when he wrote in Macbeth about plucking from the memory "a rooted sorrow." Hurtful words from a cruel tongue is something you have to live with forever whereas the painful tooth can be extracted, the operation performed, the painkiller administered and the painful experience gradually forgotten. I recently heard the words "to know all is to forgive all" so, one day, in the next world, when we see the whole picture perhaps we will understand and be able to forgive those who have caused us to suffer.

Life holds terrible sorrows for many and there is not one person who goes through their earthly life completely free from pain and anguish. You should never look with envy at someone and think what a good life they have and how lucky they are. When we read the biographies of the rich and famous we learn of the heartaches they have experienced in life. Many of our movie stars seem to change their partners so often in a continual quest for love. Even the highest in the land are not immune from suffering as we all know from the books about Princess Diana. Some of the nicest people in the world are those who have passed through painful experiences and can understand and therefore help others who are experiencing these situations. It is through suffering that we become more understanding, more sympathetic and more compassionate. Harrison Ford, the well-known actor, made a film called "Regarding Henry" about a hard-nosed New York lawyer who was shot in the head, suffered brain damage and emerged from it a much nicer person. Gordon Smith has said in his book "Spirit Messenger" that it is through our suffering that we grow. Gordon Higginson, a former president of the SNU, has written in his book "Touched by the Angels" that we all emerge from sorrow and pain a stronger person. He goes on to say that no life or experience is wasted although we cannot see the whole pattern. One day we will look back and realise that we gained strength from the whole experience. It is at times like these that we really need God "when we pass through the waters" [Isa.43:2] and indeed many people have found God in the midst of their suffering.

One of my favourite verses from the Bible (the Apocrapha) is "For gold is tried in the fire, and acceptable men in the furnace of humiliation" [Ecclesiasticus 2:5-6] or as Seneca phrased it "Fire is the test of God : adversity of strong men." Our spirit guides tell us that one day we will look back over the road of our life and realize that the things we experienced that were unpleasant at the time made us stronger. I do not understand why people are born with terrible handicaps but I do believe that there is a purpose behind everything. Stephen O'Brien, another well-known Spiritualist medium has also said this. He says that by meeting the challenge of handicap our souls grow and that we choose the body we need to progress spiritually. Here is another of my favourite quotations. (Author unknown)

"Not till the loom is silent and the shutters cease to fly,
Will God unfold the pattern and explain the reason why,
The dark threads are as needful in the weaver's skilful hands,
As the threads of gold and silver in the pattern He has planned."

I find it a comfort to know that in the next world there are wonderful compensations for those who have suffered disabilities while on earth. Every communication received from the next world speaks of freedom from former pain and suffering, whole bodies, restored vision and hearing. In short complete physical fitness. I also find it a comfort to know that each life on earth is but a second in eternity. We must remember also that what happens to the body does not also happen to the spirit. The spirit is not crippled or handicapped in any way and because you enjoy a healthy body does not mean that your spirit is better than one whose body is diseased. In fact the one who has learned the lessons of pain and suffering while on earth will be the richer in spirit.

Down through the ages physical sickness was often said to be God's punishment for sins committed. If you recovered then it was said that God had forgiven you. This idea was held very strongly in the minds of ancient people and I think that is why Jesus said to the man in the Bible before he cured him "My son, your sins are forgiven you."[Matt 9:2] Jesus knew all about "mind over matter!" Jesus in his lifetime spent a lot of time healing the sick. We are told he was "moved to pity" by the suffering he saw around him and he told his followers to go out and heal the sick. Sadly the church became obsessed with theology and healing was pushed into the background. Pope Innocent 3 condemned surgery as being contrary to God's law! It was the ancient church that destroyed the two famous medical schools in Athens and Alexandria which both possessed wonderful libraries. These were burned to the ground. What precious medical knowledge have we lost because of this act of vandalism? The church was too obsessed with saving souls to care about physical bodies. At least William Booth, the founder of the Salvation Army understood the importance of feeding men's bodies before trying to feed their minds. Spiritualist Churches have trained healers who must pass exams before they are allowed to practice. They work with the medical fraternity in the next world to try to alleviate the suffering in this world. The late Harry Edwards was one of the most famous healers of them all and if anyone doubts the reality of spiritual healing they should read his life story.

In 1951 a committee was formed by the Archbishops of Canterbury and York to investigate Spiritual healing. Of 70 incurable cases which Harry Edwards had cured they did not investigate one of them. They did not interview the patients, the patients' doctors or see the case records. Their report concluded that doctors and churchmen should unite to exorcise demons! At one time I suffered from Tinitus. The doctor was unable to help so I went to spiritual healing for 4 weeks and was completely cured. Many people think that spiritual healing is all to do with having faith but this is not so. Our healers work with doctors from the next world and the "faith" of the patient is quite irrelevant. Many animals are brought to healing clinics. Do they have faith?

I do not believe for one minute that God deliberately sends sickness to people but I do believe that it is possible to bring illness upon yourself by the lifestyle that you lead. What about drugs? What about alcohol abuse? We all know that smoking can kill by causing cancer, that obesity is responsible for a whole range of illnesses and that an immoral lifestyle can cause sexually transmitted diseases. We are told that cleanliness is next to Godliness and here again if we neglect personal hygiene we will bring diseases upon ourselves. There is no way that you can blame God for something that is self-inflicted. We must all learn to take responsibility for our own actions. Sadly these days we are all at the mercy of food manufacturers and we become ill because of all the additives and pesticides which are used to produce food. Farm animals are given injections to make their flesh leaner and cows are similarly treated to increase their milk yield. You are at the end of the food chain. As I write supermarkets across the world are removing foods contaminated with the Sudan 1 red dye which can cause cancer. It is man's free-will in running our world that causes these disasters and the consequent suffering.

Of course there are times when dreadful things happen which are not your fault. We read these days of drunken drivers mowing down innocent pedestrians walking along the pavement. Like everyone I feel a righteous anger when I read of such things and also of the lenient sentences handed out by our justice department. Our guides in the next world tell us that their ledgers are always balanced and that those who escape justice in this world will face it in the next. Then there are natural disasters like earthquakes, famine, flooding. I do not pretend to have answers to these NATURAL disasters but other disasters are caused by HUMANS. We are all part of the human family and if one section of that family acts irresponsibly then we will all suffer the consequences. If one country decides to go to war with another then we are all caught up in the consequences. God cannot interfere with the free-will which He has allowed us in this world.

I believe that for every illness on this earth there is a cure just waiting to be discovered. However I do not believe that such cures will be discovered by practising cruelties on innocent animals in medical laboratories. God will never allow good to come out of cruelty to His creatures. I also believe that many illness are caused by disharmony in the human body. The word "Disease" after all just means exactly that "Dis-ease." We all know that worry can bring on ulcers, living under constant stress and tension can cause high blood pressure. Nearly all diseases arise from states of mental disharmony. We need to live rightly and to think rightly. We need to restore serenity of mind. If we own a piece of equipment and it develops a fault then we take it back to the manufacturer. Well we need to take ourselves back to the One who created us, the One who gave us our life in the first place, the One who knows all about us and who is the greatest healer of them all.

CHAPTER 10
WHAT I BELIEVE ABOUT PRAYER.

Prayer is your own private communication channel to God and the next world. It is through this channel that you receive the strength to bear your troubles, guidance to deal with your problems and help to cope with all the experiences of your earthly life.

Prayer is not sending to God a list of things you want or would like to happen. Selfish prayers for more money or more possessions cannot be called prayer. The Bible says "Ye ask and receive not because ye ask amiss." [James 4:3] You cannot ask God to let you win the lottery! However if you desperately need a small sum of money then I believe that God will provide it. My mother told me the story of how when she was a small girl and going to the Brownies one evening she desperately needed a penny to put into the collection. Her family was terribly poor and she could not possibly ask her mother for it. She prayed to God to give her a penny for her Brownie Meeting and, walking along the road, she found an old battered penny but a real penny nevertheless which she could use. I often think of this story today when I see young people carelessly discarding coppers from their person as being too trivial to bother about. Real prayer comes from your soul. You should be opening your heart to your creator asking for His help, His strength to help you through some ordeal you have to face up to, His wisdom and guidance to deal with some difficult situation in your life and your concern for others. "Show me what I have to do and give me the strength to do it." Sincere prayer will always find its target in the next world. Again to quote from the Good Book "The effectual fervent prayer of a righteous man availeth much" [James 5:16] or, as Lord Tennyson put it [Idylls of the King] "More things are wrought by prayer than this world dreams of."

I have heard people say that they do not know how to pray. I have never had this difficulty. I talk to God in prayer as if He was, as indeed He is, my best friend. I tell Him things I would not tell another living soul. I tell Him my worries, I ask His help in living my everyday life, I petition Him on behalf of others I know are ill or have other problems. I know that God will answer the prayer in the way that is best. You may be praying for a loved one to recover from some illness and go on living when in actual fact you may be condemning them to a life they would not desire. You must pray for what is best for them and this may be to go to the next world. When we pray for someone we are bringing that person and their circumstances before God. I don't only pray for the living, I pray for the dead also! Most religions pray for their dead and so do Spiritualists. If you had a member of your family who emigrated to the other side of the world you would pray that they got there safely, that they settled into their new life and perhaps met up with some they knew who were already there. Well, this is how it is with the newly dead. They need our prayers in just the same way. I pray for the newly bereaved that they will be comforted and strengthened to carry on. I pray for world peace, I pray for the lonely, the unloved, the one who has been told that he/she is suffering from a terminal illness, the one who did not get the job offer, the one who failed the exam. There are plenty of things to pray about! I always pray for the animal kingdom that human beings will become more compassionate towards other living creatures and lastly I never forget to thank God for such blessings as I possess and receive. I think ingratitude is a terrible thing. Many people only pray when some crisis strikes their life and, once the dilemma is over, they never think to contact God again.

I can pray to God in any place and at any time. You do not need to be in a church to pray to God. What do people do who can't talk to God like this? Who do they turn to when trouble strikes — when they feel completely and utterly alone in the world? Sometimes I have sent what could be termed an "arrow" prayer to God. This is a prayer that seems to rise from the depths of my being in a moment of crisis and I have felt a sort of "tug" inside of me as if the arrow has hit its target and I know that all will be well. There is a verse in the Bible which I think describes this. [Isaiah 65:24] "Before they call I will answer and while they are yet speaking I will hear." I believe that God already knows the unspoken prayers of our hearts and He longs to give us what we need but so often we don't ask! The Letter of James in the Bible puts it this way "Ye have not because ye ask not." [James 4:2]. James was Jesus' younger brother and he would have learned such things in the family home from his big brother. If you study the gospels you will see that Jesus always said to people "what do you want me to do?" [Luke 18:41-42] He made them put their problem into words. Helen Steiner Rice who writes such wonderful inspirational poetry has put it this way — "Prayers can't be answered unless they are prayed."

What about Public Prayer? Well, Public Prayer is when one person speaks to God on behalf of a gathered group of people. Some of these prayers are wonderful and put into words what some of us would find difficulty in expressing ourselves. Prayers in Spiritualist churches are offered by the visiting mediums. He or she will often refer to topical events like national disasters, murders and other atrocities that the whole nation is concerned about. I remember when the Foot and Mouth crisis was raging that the medium prayed for the souls of the animals who had been sent with such speed into the next world. She mentioned their fear and distress and prayed that they would receive comfort and reassurance on the other side by those who would meet them. The aimless repetition of prayers recited daily which repeat words that others have written can do little good for your soul. How many people truly think about what they are saying when they repeat the Lord's prayer? There are some parts of it that I have always had difficulty with and I often think that it should be made more relevant to our present society. After all it was given to us over 2000 years ago and the world has changed greatly since then. If Jesus came back into the world today I am sure he would phrase it differently. A loving god does not "lead us into temptation!" The prayer must have lost some of its meaning in two thousand years of translation.

What about answers to prayers? Well, remember that sending a prayer to God is a bit like being on a telephone and you must listen for His answer! Prayers are always answered but perhaps not in the way that you expect. I was taught years ago that there are three answers to any prayer. YES, NO and WAIT. Our beloved Spirit Guide Silver Birch was asked why so often prayers seem to go unanswered and this was his reply.

"Sometimes you ask for things which are not good for your soul which will only retard your progress and so these things cannot be given to you. Sometimes you ask for things which your soul has not earned or for things which are already in preparation for you when the right time comes."

Jesus said "Ye know not what ye ask" [Mark 10:38] and I think we should be grateful that God does not always give us what we ask. Often we may look back over our life and think "well I wanted it at the time but now I am glad that I never got it." Let us be grateful that we have a loving God who knows what is best for us and who gives us what we need and not what we want. Remember that prayers are not always answered on your time schedule. A favourite saying of mine is "The hand that is ready, the heart that has planned." If you learn to pray for right things, in the right way then your prayer will be answered at the right time and in the best way for you. There is another quotation that I have found very relevant to prayer and that is "God's clocks keep perfect time." Many of my prayers have been answered at the last possible moment and in the nick of time, almost as if He was testing my faith. I don't believe that there is only God sitting on some throne in the next world listening to my prayers and rubber-stamping them. I believe that there is a vast organization up there who have been delegated to deal with such matters but I still pray to a personal God. I have said earlier that the God I love and worship knows all about me. Well He certainly knows that I am a Star Trek fan because one evening when starting to pray I said "Dear God" and was astounded when my clair-audient voice came right back to me saying "Hailing frequencies open!" I was so stunned I could not speak and I could almost hear the laughter in heaven!

Besides directing prayers to God I also frequently ask for help from the next world to solve my day to day problems. I have already said that the next world is peopled by those who previously lived in this world. It is filled with teachers, doctors, electricians, dress-makers and in fact every possible job, trade and profession is represented. I have never seen any reason why I could not call on this vast universe of experts for help and I am sure that they are more than delighted to share their knowledge and expertise and give help to those of us still struggling here on the earth plane. This help can come in one of two ways. Sometimes it is "earthly" helper like someone you get chatting to on a bus who will know the answer to your problem (I know the very shop which sells it. Ask the chemist to give you this for it helped me.) Other times it is an idea that suddenly just pops into your head, a memory is stirred, a line of a hymn, poem or a verse from the Bible comes to you to give you the answer. In my case sometimes my clair-audient voice comes through. There is one occasion which I will never forget when this happened. I was moving home, doing everything myself and struggling to pull nails out of a carpet. I was trying to do it by levering them out with a screwdriver and tugging them out with pliers. I reached the point when I just could not get some of them out and, being absolutely at the end of my tether I started to cry. I sat on the floor and sobbed "somebody, help me help me." The voice came with utmost clarity. "You are holding the pliers the wrong way. See that hole in the middle? Wrap the hole round the nail and tug upwards." I followed the instruction and the nails came out easily. Was it my father in the next world or was it some helpful joiner who came to my assistance? I don't know but I was so grateful to that person.

I don't think we should ask God or the next world for something and then sit back and wait for it to happen. I am a strong believer in the saying that "God helps those who help themselves." If I have a problem then I will try and solve it myself before I turn to God. Then I can honestly say "I've done my best Lord God, now I really need your help." Dr Billy Graham has said that "worry is a sin. It shows a lack of trust in God" but I am afraid that I am one of the world's great worriers. Having worried myself sick about some problem I remember the phrase "let go and let God" and I mentally hand my burden over feeling a sense of relief that it is up to God now and of course He sorts out the problem as if He had just been waiting for me to ask!

CHAPTER 11
WHAT I BELIEVE ABOUT THE BIBLE.

I had always wanted to read the Bible and really understand it but I had been put off by the old fashioned language used and having nobody to really explain it to me. Nowadays we have many versions of the Bible written in our everyday language which should overcome part of the problem. I had of course learned all the usual Bible stories while a child but I wanted more than this. I never understood what happened between the time that Jesus supposedly rose from the dead and me going to a Sunday School 2000 years later. No one ever told me about the growth of the early church and it was years before I learned of the efforts of the disciples to spread the teachings of Jesus and to start the first Christian Churches.

I really started to study and understand the Bible properly when I joined a Bible study group in the YWCA. We were a very small group but enthusiastic and, having discovered the commentaries by Dr William Barclay, we worked our way through nearly all the New Testament using these commentaries. These opened up the Bible for me as never before and I will always regret that he never lived to do something similar for the Old Testament. However there is no way I believe every single word which is written in the Bible. We are told that the world was peopled by Adam and Eve but, as they only had three sons, who did these sons marry in order to produce children? Something similar happens in the story of Noah although his sons did have wives. Who did his grandchildren marry? —their cousins? Medical science would not agree with this today as it would produce in-breeding. Well, maybe that explains the crazy world we live in!

While I believe that God created me I prefer the scientific theory that all life has evolved over millions of years from a common source. Scientists now know that we have many genes in common with the animal kingdom and indeed I have just read that we share 99% of our genes with chimpanzees. Someone said to a guide from the next world that he did not like the idea that he was related to monkeys. I just loved the reply he was given. "The monkeys are not too keen on the idea either!"

So — what do Spiritualists think about the Bible? In the words of our beloved Silver Birch "it is a mixture of divine truth and man's falsification." We are told not to blindly accept any teaching that goes against our reasoning. Well, a great many things in the Bible go against my reasoning! I have read that it is a guidebook for my life, a handbook for my salvation and that I must live by its principles. There are passages and verses from the Bible which I really love but there are large parts of it that I just cannot believe and I am sure that there are others like me all over the world. There are some passages in the Old Testament which cannot possibly be from God because they revolt us and go against every instinct of justice. For example the Bible tells you that it is acceptable to go out and slaughter and pillage. This is certainly not the word of a God of love! Many Christians try to uphold the statements in the Bible no matter how absurd they all are. We speak of the "Gospel Truth" but the gospels can be very far from the truth. Many gospels which contained the original teachings of Jesus were banned and destroyed by the early church because they disagreed with the views expressed in them. Censorship was practised even then! Now Jesus was a well-educated man. He read the scriptures in the synagogue but if he ever wrote anything down then it has been suppressed. Modern Christianity is based on the teachings of Paul who never knew Jesus. He ignored the wonderful teachings of Jesus and substituted pagan teachings about a god who used the death of Jesus as a sacrifice for the sins of the people. Dedicated followers of Jesus have also written about him but, in their anxiety to make him appear as a Saviour God they have distorted and invented some happenings. An example of this is the feeding of the 5000.[John 6: 1-14]. The miracle here was not of the multiplication of food but of the opening of the human heart when, shamed by the little boy offering his mother's packed lunch to Jesus, others in the crowd produced their own packed lunches and offered to share them with those who had neglected to bring with them something to eat. I believe in miracles but these miracles happen in a perfectly natural way and cynics would sneer and call them coincidences. The following story is now found on the Internet but I read it many years ago on Francis Gay's page in the Scottish Sunday Post. A little girl lay dying in a very poor home and the doctor said to her mother that only a miracle could save her. The child's brother who heard this ran out the house to the local chemist and asked to buy a miracle as it was the only thing that could save his little sister's life. He thought it was some kind of medication. However standing in the shop was a famous doctor and, hearing the little lad's tale, he went home with him and with his skill he saved the life of the little girl. That to me was a miracle. Here is another example of God working a miracle. A colleague of mine was engaged to a veterinary surgeon. While enjoying a drive out in the country they noticed a bird fluttering at the side of the road in great distress. Stopping the car my colleague's fiancee got out to see what was wrong and he discovered that the bird had dislocated its wing. With a couple of clicks of his skilful, trained fingers he sorted the problem and the bird was able to fly away. Only God could arrange that a vet be driving past that spot at that time. Many will have heard the tale of the gardener burning bonfires of rubbish in his garden and having great difficulty in getting one of the fires to light up. He opened out the heap to see what was stopping the flames and discovered a bird with her wings stretched protectively across a nest containing her little ones. Another miracle of the love of God —"not a sparrow shall fall." Spiritualists don't believe in miracles. We believe that everything that happens is in accordance with natural laws some of which we still have not discovered. Two thousand years ago televisons, mobile phones and computers would all have been considered miraculous but we today just accept them. What we consider miraculous today (eg communication with the next world) will be accepted as normal by our descendants.

Single words and expressions in the Bible have been drawn completely out of context. Think of the saying "money is the root of all evil." This is a misquotation for the verse "The love of money is the root of all evil." There is nothing wrong with money and a great deal of good can be done in the world by wealthy people. It is the mean Scrooges of the world that the Bible is here condemning. Jesus certainly did not agree with the way the Jewish Pharisees interpretated the scriptures. They told him off for healing on the Sabbath and he replied that the Sabbath was made for man and not man for the Sabbath. I wonder what he would think if he came back to the world today and read our modern Bible. Maybe he would say "I never said that!" As far as the Old Testament is concerned we should remember that it was written for a particular race and nation — the Hebrew people and reflects their history and culture. It just cannot be applied to us today. I don't believe for one moment that God told them to go out and kill. It would be their High Priests who did this for they claimed to know the will of God just as the Pope claims to do so today. An article in the "Two Worlds" monthly magazine really highlighted some of the more ridiculous verses of the Bible. Exodus 21:7 says to sell your daughter into slavery while 35:2 says that anyone who works on the Sabbath should be put to death. What about all the lives that our dedicated medics are saving on that day of the week? The book of Leviticus also has some gems of wisdom. Lev. 19:27 forbids getting hair trimmed around the temples, 21:20 says you should not approach the altar if you have a defect in your eyesight (so that cuts out all the blind as well as anyone who wears spectacles) while 25:44 says that it is ok to possess slaves. Oh William Wilberforce you did not read your Bible when you persuaded the British government to abolish the slave trade! The above are only a few examples from the "Good Book" which we are told to accept as the word of God. If that is the God that the churches are telling us to worship then I want nothing to do with him. My God is a god of love who would never have said things like that.

Revelation from God is ongoing. God did not speak to His people over 2000 years ago and has kept silent ever since. God reveals His truths to us according to our ability to understand. We must remember that new revelations will come through a human channel (an inspired one) and therefore they may be subject to human error. If your reason accepts what is in the Bible then that is fine but if not reject it or else put it to one side awaiting further understanding.

The Bible has been written and changed many times to suit man and it is full of discrepancies and contradictions. Modern Biblical research and modern discoveries prove that much previously accepted truths are not so. The Emperor Constantine in the year 326 ordered that all books holding views that differed from the official teachings should be destroyed and this practice has continued over the centuries. Church fathers have modified it for their own benefit. There is only one reference in the Bible to reincarnation and yet it was a widely held belief in the ancient world and indeed today it is still believed by over half the earth's population. The reason is that the church did not want people to believe that they had more than one chance of getting into Heaven!

The trouble is that people have changed and added to the Bible over the centuries and God's words have been mixed up with texts of their own making. The New Testament was not put together until 300 years after Jesus died so we don't know the correct facts. Before printing was invented Biblical texts were copied out by hand by scribes. So — the Bible is a copy of a copy of a copy.........! These texts had been translated from Aramaic, into Hebrew, into Greek and then into Latin! That alone accounts for a lot of mistakes. There would be a roomful of scribes with a leader who would be dictating to them. If this leader had poor eyesight then he could easily dictate incorrectly. If one of the scribes had poor hearing then he could easily write down the wrong word. Bad handwriting would also account for mistakes for the next generation of scribes. All of these mistakes would be copied, recopied and even more mistakes would creep in. Years ago I worked in a large city library system. If something important needed to be communicated to all the staff it was sent around the libraries by what was referred to as a "Rotation Message." The message started off from the main library and was telephoned to the first on the list where it was written down and then telephoned on to the next library on the list and so on. Eventually it was repeated back to the main library from where it had started. The final message to be passed on was seldom identical to the one which had started out. Bits had been missed out and bits put in and the whole thing had to be gone over again to correct the discrepancies. Now if something like that can happen in just about one hour, imagine what can happen in over 2000 years! I repeat I cannot believe every single word that is in the Bible.

There are wise and spiritual teachings within the scriptures of all faiths. All such teachings should be in accordance with one another if they are truly inspired from God. There is only one God for everyone. He has spoken to His people in many ways and through many different voices. It is time that all such spiritual teachings be studied and brought together in one comprehensive volume for the benefit of God's people. Then we really would have a guidebook for our life.

CHAPTER 12
WHAT I BELIEVE ABOUT THE ANIMAL KINGDOM.

Mahatma Ghandi said "The greatness of a nation can be judged by the way its animals are treated." The same spirit from God which is part of all of us is also present in all the creatures who share this planet with us. I believe that He cares just as much for the sparrow who hops on the ground as He does for you and me. Jesus spoke of this fact when he said that not a sparrow falls to the ground but God is aware of it. Why is God aware of it? Because the sparrow within it's tiny body contains the divine spark of God and whenever anything happens to the sparrow, God feels a tug as if from an invisible thread. We are all attached to God in this way and because of this God knows everything that happens to us. Everyone should understand that if they murder or hurt a living creature in any way that hurt is felt by God Himself. All living creatures on earth have a life span which should be lived naturally from start to finish. God gave life to all and only God has the right to call his creatures back when their time on earth is over.

Mankind must learn to co-exist with all other life forms. They are not here for us to use as food, as clothing, to practise experiments on or to be used for entertainment. Man is also an animal and he may be at the top of the creative ladder but he still has a very long way to go when it comes to kindness and compassion. Are human beings superior to animals? I sometimes wonder. Animals kill for food. They do not indulge in so called blood sports. If we are truly superior to animals then we have a responsibility towards them because the higher should always help the lower. Animals have as much right to be on this earth as human beings and mankind must learn to acknowledge the right of all other species to share this planet with us. The lack of compassion towards animals is a shameful blot on the history of civilization. It is incredible that animal and bird welfare organizations have to buy up tracts of land to provide a permanent habitat for birds and animals but they will have to to do this if mankind continues to needlessly cut down trees, bushes, forests and otherwise destroy places which are home to other earth dwellers.

Millions of people on this earth have no compassion or understanding for the animal kingdom. They look on them as "just animals" put on the earth for their own convenience or material gain. However things are improving and programmes like "Animal Hospital" and "Pet Rescue" have helped to make us all more aware of how alike we all are. Like us, animals have feelings, emotions and memories. Like us they feel pain, stress and terror. We should respect all other forms of God's creation. Life is sacred. It comes from God. It is entitled to be treated with sacredness and should not be held cheaply. You have no power to create life therefore you should not seek to destroy it. The Law of Islam forbids killing animals for fun or sport. It also forbids letting an animal go hungry, beating it or putting an intolerable burden on it. The Hindu view is that "The wise should not act sinfully towards animals or cause others to act so." Buddhists say "The higher type of man treats animals with kindness." while the Book of Proverbs (12:10) says "A righteous man cares for the need of his animals." Is it not time that the Christian Churches said something about animal rights?

The Christian Church is largely responsible for our attitude towards animals. It does not teach that we should respect other creatures as our spiritual kith and kin. The church teaches that only humans have souls and so, if animals have no souls, there is no guilt in killing them. How strange that they should have forgotten the teachings of their founder about love and compassion. Can you imagine Jesus treating any animal with cruelty? Of course there are always exceptions like St Francis of Assisi. Many churches these days hold "animal blessing services" in which members of the congregation bring their pets to church. I wonder how many go home after the service and sit down to eat roast lamb, roast chicken, roast beef, pork chops etc. Man was not placed in the world to eat animals and all true spiritualists today are vegetarians. This decision not to eat animals is something that your own soul must decide on. It depends on your own evolvement and spiritual progression. You yourself must reach the understanding that "it is wrong to extinguish another's life in order to sustain your own" (Silver Birch) and Gandhi has said "Spiritual progress does demand at some stage that we should cease to kill our fellow creatures for the satisfaction of our bodily wants." In the undeveloped world it is not always possible to have this ideal but in any civilized country it is perfectly possible to maintain a healthy diet and lifestyle as a vegetarian. Indeed scientists tell us that vegetarians are much healthier than meat eaters and less subject to illnesses of all sorts. Many people think that they must eat meat to give them strength. They should remember that horses, oxen, bulls, and elephants are all vegetarian. Look what happened when cows were fed the minced up remains of other animals! It was the start of "Mad Cow Disease" or "variant CJD" as it is called in humans. Don't blame God for this disease! Man brings such things upon himself by his method of living. Many people today are increasingly subject to food intolerances. Livestock are injected with various drugs to make them fatter, leaner and increase their milk yield. Any such substances will eventually reach the human who consumes that animal. Again it is man who has brought about such illnesses. Don't blame God! This is the spiritual Law of Cause and Effect.

All animals experience fear and pain. Can you imagine the fear of animals entering slaughter houses and abattoirs? They can smell the blood of their own kind. This is very different from "putting to sleep" a beloved pet. If you eat flesh you must first extinguish the life of the animal and you must therefore assume this responsibility. How many readers of this book would kill in order to eat? Not many, I think. We prefer to buy it ready packaged for us and when we buy it like this do we think at all about the animal whose life has been extinguished. Do we realize that "bacon" "sausage" and even the word "meat" means animals. As a child I did not realize that when I was given meat to eat that I was actually consuming an animal. It was only as I got older that I realized with horror exactly what "Roast Lamb" was. I remember I felt physically sick when I realized what "Tongue" was. To this day I always avert my face as I walk past a meat counter or butcher's shop and I remember being in Marks and Spencers one day before Christmas and feeling as if I was in a mortuary as I saw all the corpses of chickens and turkeys laid out to buy for Christmas meals. Silver Birch has said in one of his books "what a pity that the birth of the Prince of Peace (Jesus) is commemorated by such dreadful slaughter. That the blood of innocent creatures has to flow in order to commemorate peace. It is a holocaust of bloodshed by needless sacrifices of dumb creatures." Experts in the Spirit World suggest that the eating of flesh meat of any description should be gradually reduced and finally abandoned altogether. It is not a good idea to become an overnight vegetarian for, if your body has been used to meat, it will not take kindly to a sudden change of diet. I myself have not eaten meat for over 25 years although I still eat some fish. I find it difficult when eating out as hotels and restaurants seem to think that vegetarians are happy to eat curries, pastas and other foreign style meals covered with spices. It seems impossible for them to provide you with a Quorn meal (very similar to chicken) or any other "meat" alternative. However we are lucky in the UK in that our prepackaged food is clearly marked "suitable for vegetarians." On holidays in the USA and Canada I was disappointed to see that their food had no such labels.

Hunting animals for pleasure is an obscenity. The XLV Dalai Lama has said "Killing animals for sport, for pleasure and for hides and furs is a phenomenon which is disgusting and distressing. There is no such justification in indulging in such acts of brutality." Beautiful birds are shot in the name of sport. We have outlawed bear-baiting and cock-fighting and please God we will outlaw fox hunting also. Imagine a stag or a fox chased by hounds that have been incited by the blood lust of humankind. Imagine that creature's fear. Let no one be in doubt that if they practise cruelty against any animal then they will answer for it in the next world. I have heard people speak of certain animals as "Vermin." Do they realize that they are accusing God of creating vermin? I have never liked to see animals in zoos although I can see the need for them where the species is endangered. I have never liked circuses which I always felt were "making a fool of animals." To see the King of the Jungle made to sit on a stool or jump through a hoop is shameful. Let us treat all animals with the dignity they are entitled to as part of God's creation.

When human beings donate blood or organs for transplant such an action is with their consent and is given with love. However no animal gives its consent to have its organs used by humans. Animals should not be regarded as spare parts for human transplants. An animal to human transplant is totally repugnant. I remember when I learned that an acquaintance had had a pig's valve put in her heart. I was absolutely horrified and vowed that such a thing would never happen to me. I would rather be dead than walk around with part of an animal's body inside of me but then — I am not afraid to die! Perhaps if others lost their fear of death they would not think it necessary to preserve their life at any cost.

Animals also do not consent to have abominable operations performed on them in the name of science. "Can there be any worse spiritual crime than inflicting deliberate harm on a fellow creature" [Silver Birch]. Vivisection is wrong. It is cruel, needless and fails to achieve its object. Scientists use animals for experiments because they desire to help humanity. They hope to gain knowledge which will help to conquer disease. Their motives may be sincere but God will never allow good to come out of cruelty to animals. Look what thalidomide did to the world! Many years ago there was a picture in (I think) Picture Post or Life magazine of two monkeys in a cage in an animal laboratory. They had their skinny little arms wrapped around one another in their fear and terror. That photo has haunted me all my life. I am ashamed to live in a country that allows such terrible things to happen to other living creatures. Animals were not placed here by God to be used in experiments to prolong the physical life of man. "Just because a life form is different from your own does not mean that it is expendable."[Star Trek TNG].

Vain and shallow women of the world have been responsible for much cruelty to animals with their idea that "fur is beautiful." I have read that 35 million animals are killed each year to satisfy the fur trade. Wild animals are caught by the use of cruel traps and fur factories breed animals in intolerable conditions. Do women think when they speak of their "mink" coats, their "fox furs" their "sable muffs", their "leopard skin coats" their "squirrel" hats, etc of the animal killed for the garment? I read years ago of a little boy who was psychically gifted who called his mother's fur coat, the coat that cried. He could sense the pain of the original owner of that coat and I have been at spiritualist meetings years ago where the medium would not give a message to anyone wearing a fur coat. Thankfully we do not see as many fur coats today and many furriers shops are closing down but the trade has not been defeated yet. I do like to see fur trims on clothes but surely it is possible to use imitation fur. I would never buy a garment which contained real fur and I have only contempt for any woman who wears fur in this day and age. It is a pity that our royal family and our pop stars and other human icons who wield so much power over their fans cannot use their influence for good in this direction. An article in the Daily Mail has highlighted the recent popularity of using snakeskins as a fashion accessory and tells of the horrific methods used to kill snakes, alligators, pythons, crocodiles etc. It is stomach churning. God does not want animals slaughtered so that their carcases can be used for the adornment of the human body. Cosmetics is another area where cruelty is practised on animals. We have all read of rabbits having shampoos dripped into their eyes. Thankfully these days it is possible to buy items which have not been tested on animals. If every woman in the land said that in future she would not buy any item which had resulted from cruelty to animals then we could soon bring about a change for the better.

One question which many people ask of Spiritualists is about beloved pets who have died. The church's teaching is that man was made in the image of God (how does anyone know what God looks like?) and that only man can survive death. This must bring a great deal of anguish to those mourning for a beloved pet and it is completely untrue! Every living creature is animated by the same spirit of God as you and I. Many, many times in Spiritualist meetings I have heard the medium refer to the owner's pets in the next world. I remember one church meeting where a member of the congregation was being told of family members in the next world who had gathered to greet her. The medium was giving out the names and she said to her "they are telling me that Glen is with them but I don't know who they mean." "Oh" said the recipient" "that's our dog." How nice to know that the dog was still with his family in the next world. I have also heard a message from the next world where the the medium said that the communicator was surrounded by birds - canaries, budgies etc. The person to whom the message was addressed confirmed that her father had kept cage birds all his life. "Well" said the medium "he still has them all here." Where there is deep love between an animal and it's master or mistress then that animal will still be a companion to them in the next world.

What about wild animals? When wild animals return to the spirit world they go to a group soul for they are not individuals like humans however, if they have had a special relationship with a human, then they also can return to greet a loved person. At one never to be forgotten Spiritualist meeting I was at, the medium, in complete astonishment, said that he had a monkey who wished to make contact! You can imagine the titters from the audience! The person addressed however confirmed that he had worked overseas and that he knew of the monkey. At the end of the meeting I spoke to him about this amazing message and he told me that he had a photo of the little creature at home and that he was holding him in his arms. Well I don't know which overseas country the little monkey belonged to but one Sunday morning he came to a Spiritualist meeting in the North-East of Scotland to be remembered to a human being he felt affection for. Truly, love can overcome every barrier.

Every living creature comes to earth for a purpose — that is the law of nature — and when it has served that purpose it goes home to spirit. It is wrong to think that just because you were born a human being that you are one of a supreme race and that all other living creatures are here to serve you. We are all here to share with one another. Every life has a purpose and the life of other living creatures is just as important to them as yours is to you. Every life form has a contribution to make to the world. All species are required for some purpose and none should be exterminated. Of all creatures on this earth, man is the most destructive. Without compassion there will be no spiritual progress and man is holding back his own evolution. Respect the animal kingdom as part of God's creation.

CONCLUSION

To many people the word "Spiritualism" means just one thing — talking to the dead. Recent TV programmes have encouraged this idea and this really angers me and I am sure many other spiritualists feel the same. My religion is very important to me and I do not like to see it treated as a form of popular entertainment.

Yes, we do communicate with our loved ones in the next world but that is only one part of our whole religious movement. The idea of contacting the dead has always been a subject of mockery in books and plays going right back to Madame Arcati in Noel Coward's "Blithe Spirit." Let me put the record straight. Spiritualists do not meet up in darkened rooms, sit around a table holding hands while one of the company utters moans, rolls about in a so-called trance and says "Is anyone there?" This is a load of utter rubbish! It frightens off genuine enquirers and brings our whole religion into disrepute. If anyone wants to contact a loved one in the next world I would urge them to visit a Spiritualist Church (and there are many such churches all over the world), start attending the Church services, become aware of the different visiting mediums and enquire about a private reading with one they feel is good. Of course you have to pay for these private readings — £15-£20 which will include a cassette tape of the reading — and most of the money will go towards the church funds. This is a one-to-one meeting with your chosen medium, it will last for 20 to 30 minutes and will be held in a small (well-lit!) room attached to the main church. You will probably be one of a number of such enquirers booked in for a reading so others will be there either before you or after you. I have had some wonderful evidence given to me in private readings but I have also had some that I could not accept at all so don't be put off by one "Bad" reading!

The most important message that Spiritualists try to spread is that of the power of love. At a Spiritualist Church service we are asked to "send our love to the platform" as this will enable the medium to make contact with those in the next world. All prayers in a service end with the words "these things we ask in Your name which is love." We are told that our friends and relations return to us on the the "vibration of love." Magnus, the guide of Colin Fry, says that we must all practice "unconditional love." This can be very difficult! It is easy to love those who love you and also those people who have attractive personalities. It is very hard to love unpleasant people who have turned bitter after life's disappointments and hardships. We may shudder with disgust at the dirty beggar in the street and the swaying drunk who has lost all his dignity, yet Spiritualism

teaches that each and everyone is precious in the eyes of God who knows all about us and what made us turn out the way we did. Maternal love is a great example of this for true love is blind and does not see the faults and ugliness that the eyes of others perceive. The Bible is filled with references to love and most people are familiar with the famous passage from chaper 13 of Corinthians which is often used at marriage services" ....and the greatest of these is love." Jesus said "love one another as I have loved you" [John 13:34] and love is not confined to humans. The story of Greyfriars Bobby who slept every night on his master's grave in Greyfriars Kirkyard is an outstanding example of the love which exists between animals and humans. Does anyone honestly believe that Bobby would not be reunited with his beloved master when he too passed to the next world? God would not be so cruel! At a low point in my life I was given (clair-audiently) the verse "I have loved thee with an everlasting love" [Jer. 31:3] a verse I did not recognise at that time and which I had to look up in a Bible concordance. Everyone wants to feel loved, wanted and needed and if someone reading this book feels that they have no one in the world to love them, let them be assured that God loves them. He always has and He always will. If you have no one else to live your life for in this world then live if for God and make Him proud of you.

I am a Spiritualist because I believe in the teachings of Spiritualism which make absolute sense to me. God is my father. He made the Laws of Life and the rules for living it. All humankind are my family and I regard the animal kingdom as part of my "greater" family. God gave me life but also gave me the free will to live that life as I choose. There is guidance from the next world which I can accept or reject. If I break God's laws then I must answer for the consequences and I cannot progress spiritually until I have repented and made restitution for the wrongs I have done. However many sins I commit God will never reject me and I will be given endless chances to try again.

Spiritualists know where they came from, why they are here and where they are going to when their earthly life ends. They know that they must take responsibility for what they have done with their time on the earth and that they must face up to the consequences of their actions. They know that they have all eternity stretching ahead of them to make amends, to fulfil unsatisfied aims and ambitions and to eventually experience the joys of paradise. They know that they worship a God whose love is unending, whose mercy is unlimited and who desires only the happiness and well-being of His creation.

That's why I am a Spiritualist!